WELCOME TO

V.I.P. *Membership*

Mapsco V.I.P. Members receive:

- Internet or phone access to new street information
- View updated Mapsco maps
- Zip code and city/county boundary information
- Free Mapsco online mapping
- Receive a 10% discount at any Mapsco Map & Travel Center including mapsco.com*

Online Mapping Now Available!

© Mapsco, Inc.

Additional packages available, call for more information.

P9-DZL-660

MAPSCO®
STREET GUIDE & DIRECTORY

Louisville

8TH EDITION

A ROUTING AND DELIVERY SYSTEM FOR THE GREATER LOUISVILLE AREA

VISIT US ONLINE AT www.mapsco.com

Call MAPSCO CUSTOMER CONNECTION Toll Free at (866) 277-7264 for updated street information. 8:00 AM - 5:00 PM Monday thru Friday

Please have your membership number available

ONLINE MAPPING AVAILABLE AT MAPSCO.COM

PUBLISHED BY MAPSCO, INC. 4181 CENTURION WAY ADDISON, TX 75001 (972) 450-9300

LOUISVILLE MAP - 30003

PRINTED IN CANADA

Table of Contents:

About MAPSCO®

MAPSCO History

MAPSCO originated as an outgrowth of a flower delivery business. Prior to the mid-1940s, the thought of producing maps had not entered the mind of Boyd Keith. He was too busy with his chain of Dallas flower shops. As his business grew, however, one recurring problem always presented a hurdle in his efforts to service his customers quickly and efficiently. Despite his efforts, Mr. Keith could not obtain an up-to-date map of the expanding Dallas street system. As a result, orders were delayed or cancelled.

In an effort to solve his delivery problems, Mr. Keith and his store manager, Lily Kendrick, designed, researched, drafted, indexed and finally produced a Dallas Street Guide in the early 1950s. It was originally used just for Mr. Keith's own business needs, but as soon as other delivery personnel saw it, they wanted their own. In subsequent years the guide was improved as more people requested copies.

MAPSCO, Inc. first mapped the Louisville area in 1985. Since then, MAPSCO has continually revised and updated its Louisville map base in its efforts to produce the most up-to-date maps for the area. MAPSCO's 8th edition Louisville Street Guide is the first Louisville Mapsco to be produced digitally and will provide for even more complete mapping and updates. Today MAPSCO produces Street Guides, wall maps, fold maps, software and custom maps for the Dallas, Fort Worth, Austin, San Antonio, and El Paso, Texas areas, Louisville, Kentucky, Las Cruces and Alamogordo, New Mexico and Denver, Colorado. MAPSCO also has a chain of retail Map & Travel Centers, with stores located in Addison, Dallas, Frisco, Fort Worth, Austin, and San Antonio, Texas and Denver, Colorado.

MAPSCO Personnel

Lee Ritchie, *President*

Tracy Eubanks,
Executive Vice President
Chief Operating Officer

Jim L. Morris
Vice President
Chief Financial Officer

ACCOUNTING
Paul Babb
Cynthia Lankford
LaTasha Mack
Neil Mathur
Norma A. Moya
Randy Pherigo
Gwendolyn Pruet
Tracey Smith
James Sublett

CARTOGRAPHY
Ellen Arthurs
Jason Basquin
Jim Calhoun
Steve Collins
Brad Eastlick
Jose Espinoza
Patricio Garcia
David D. Halliday
Michael M. Harris
Carmen Jacobe
Patrick Lewis
Linda McDuffie
Michael Phalen
Howard Pieratt
Thomas Pitts
Julia Prokop
Petrea Rasmussen
Elizabeth T. Scherer
Curt Shaffer
Anna Timmons
Robert Trager
Armando Villarreal
Robert S. Vinson
Anthony Zerhusen

ADMINISTRATION
Jimmie Buyers
Georgia Carnine
Trent Owens

IS
Mike Laabs
Michael Morrow
Dwight Shumate

MARKETING/ COMMUNICATIONS
Kelli Freeman
Pam Goodman
Mark Jaggers

PUBLISHING/SALES
Michael Albright
Teresa Allen
Steve Campbell
David W. Dealy
Thomas B. Ferguson
Gordon Garza-Pena
Kevin Geary
Dennis Howard
George B. Jones
Garee W. Munger
Rick Narvais
Elizabeth T. Scherer

RETAIL
Hans Arriaga
Tracey Berry
Stacey Block
Bruce E. Brown
Dee Gartland
Jarrett Gibbs
John D. Girvan
Patrick D. Greigo
David Hadovsky
Tracie Lynn Hall
Kevin Harper
Brian G. Harrelson
David W. Hatcher
Sara Hayden
Roland A. Holtz
Olivia Hurtado
John P. Isbell
Larry G. Kasner
Raymond A. Lewis
Mitch Meadows
Karla Miller
JuAune Mooney
Ronald Moore
Dorothy Moorman
Lindsay Norris
Jesus Perez
Tona C. Priddy
Hersel Sanders
Ricardo Santillan Jr.
Andrea Schark
Theresa Schulz
Jeff Shiffer
Fran Sparks-Fuller
Calvin L. Stout
Cayetana Toledo
Roberta Tower
Helen Willson
John Wistl
Joe Woodward

MAPSCO CUSTOMER CONNECTION
Lisa Patterson
Tomeki Roberson
Jennie Smith
Marcie Wade

WAREHOUSE/ DISTRIBUTION
Michael Cross
Ida Lemos
Tracy Stewart

EXPLANATION of MAP SYMBOLS

Interstate Highway Number	71	State Boundary	— - — - —
U.S. Highway Number	31	County Boundary	
State Highway Number	62	Municipal Boundary	
State Secondary Highway Number	1931	Zip Code	40243
Freeway	SNYDER	City Hall	CH
Major Arterial	JACKSON ST	Chamber of Commerce	CC
Secondary Street	GRINSTEAD	Point of Interest	●
Residential Street	OLIVE	Hospital	✚
Private Street	Bardmoor Ct	Post Office	PO
One Way Street	→	High School	HS
Bridge		Junior High School	JH
Block Number	17	Middle School	MS
Under Construction		Elementary School	ES
Railroad	CSX RR	Other School Facility	
Lake		School Administration Building	■
River/Creek		College / University	☆
Dam		Mall / Shopping Center	
Incorporated Cities		Airport	
Unincorporated Areas		Cemetery	
Municipal Name	LOUISVILLE	Park / Golf Course	

LIST of ABBREVIATIONS

AVE	Avenue	EXPWY	Expressway	PL	Place
BLVD	Boulevard	FRWY	Freeway	RD	Road
CIR	Circle	HWY	Highway	S	South
CT	Court	LN	Lane	ST	Street
DR	Drive	N	North	W	West
E	East	PKWY	Parkway		

THE FINEST, MOST COMPREHENSIVE
STREET MAP AND REFERENCE GUIDE AVAILABLE
FOR THE LOUISVILLE METROPOLITAN AREA

The Louisville MAPSCO BOOK has been continuously revised and published since 1985. MAPSCO not only serves its customers' basic need for up-to-date street maps, but also provides an effective resource tool with its comprehensive Numerical/Alphabetical Street Index with Zip Codes, and convenient lists of Major Buildings, Emergency Clinics, Public Schools and Shopping Centers.

HOW TO USE MAPSCO

COMPOSITE MAP: Shows areas into which Louisville has been divided and the map number assigned to each area. Also shown are major streets which may be used for travel from one area to another. The Composite Map appears on pages 8-11.

DIRECTORY OF STREETS: Numerical/Alphabetical listings of all streets in Jefferson county, Kentucky and listings for selected areas of the following counties: Bullitt (KY), Hardin (KY), Oldham (KY), Shelby (KY), Spencer (KY), Clarke (IN), Floyd (IN) and Harrison (IN).

TYPICAL LISTINGS

STREET NAME	CITY or COUNTY	MAPSCO GRID	ZIP CODE	BLOCK RANGE
①	②	③	④	⑤
BROOKSIDE DR . . . . .Louisville		**149Z**	40205	2300-2699
BROOKSIDE DR . . . . . .Floyd Co		**106U**	47150	3900-3999
BROOKSIDE DR . .Jeffersontown		**172R**	40299	10800-10899

Each listing is comprised of:

① **Street Name**
② **City or county in which the street is located.**
③ **MAPSCO Grid**   Area Map Number and Grid Letter needed to locate street name on map.
④ **Zip Code**   Indicates appropriate Zip Code for block ranges shown.
⑤ **Block Range**   Indicates the range of street address block numbers shown on the map.

The number 149 of the first example indicates area map number. The letter Z indicates a grid. Each map is divided into 24 sections (or grids), outlined in color, and each grid is assigned a letter for identification, also shown in the same color. To locate BROOK-SIDE DR.., turn to Area Map 149. A quick glance at the grid lettered Z will show you the location of Brookside Dr. on the map. The zip code for the first listing of block numbers is 40205; the second is 40299. The numbers 2300-2699 indicate the range of blocks of Brookside Dr. on map 149.

The other two examples show other streets in Greater Louisville named Brookside Dr.

ALPHABETIZATION FORMAT
MAPSCO utilizes a strict alphabetical system which places each street in sequence based on the first letter of the first name of the street. Each subsequent letter of the street name *(except for the "Suffix")* is then used without regard to punctuation, abbreviation or spacing between words to further place the street in its appropriate order. The "Suffix" *(i.e. Ave, Ct, Frwy, Ln...etc.)* is then used as the next level of alphabetization. When two or more streets are spelled exactly the same, including the "suffix", the city of Louisville entry is shown first *(if one exists)* then all subsequent streets are placed in alphabetical order based on the name of the city in which the street is located.

AREA MAPS:
These area maps include all streets incorporated in Greater Louisville. These area maps also include all streets in Charlestown, Georgetown and Sellersburg, Indiana as well as streets in La Grange, Mt. Washington, Shelbyville, Simpsonville and Shepherdsville, Kentucky. The area maps are numbered in sequences of fourteen beginning with maps 63 through 76. The next sequence is 85 through 96. This sequential numbering allows for expansion for the area of coverage. On the margin of each area map, the adjoining map *(if one exists)* is indicated by the reference "Continued on Map_____". This allows you to readily locate the required map area when a street extends from one map area to another. Street address block numbers have been placed on most major streets at intervals, and in many cases on other streets to facilitate the location of specific sections of streets.

MAPSCO ROUTING AND DELIVERY SYSTEM:
A very effective and expedient delivery system that will solve routing and delivery problems for business firms servicing the city and its environs with package deliveries or service calls. Incoming calls and orders are plotted on a master Wall Map. Service can be dispatched by map and grid number located in the MAPSCO Book. By utilizing the MAPSCO Wall Map and MAPSCO Street Guide to its full potential you can save valuable time and money.

LOUISVILLE AREA MAP

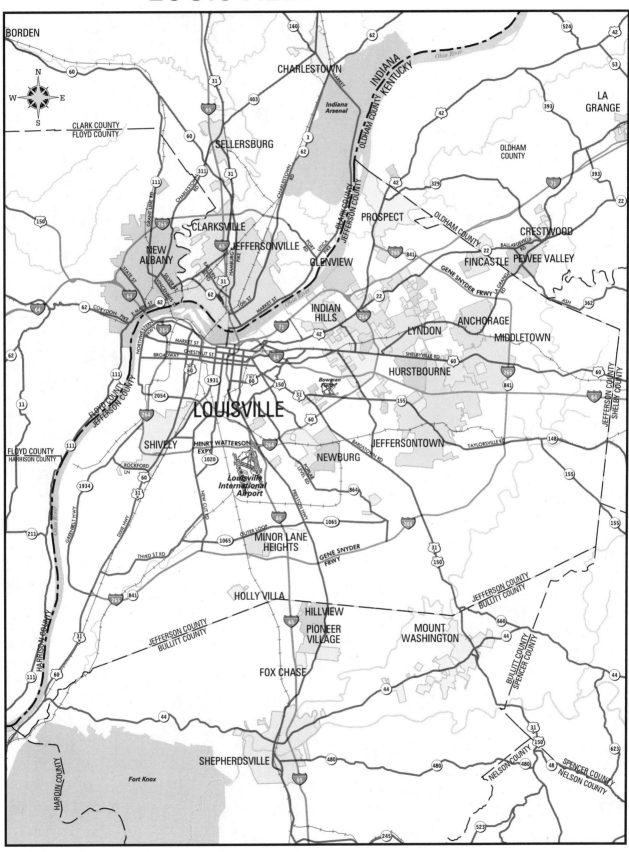

SCALE 1 Inch = 4.45 Miles

NORTHWEST AREA COMPOSITE MAP

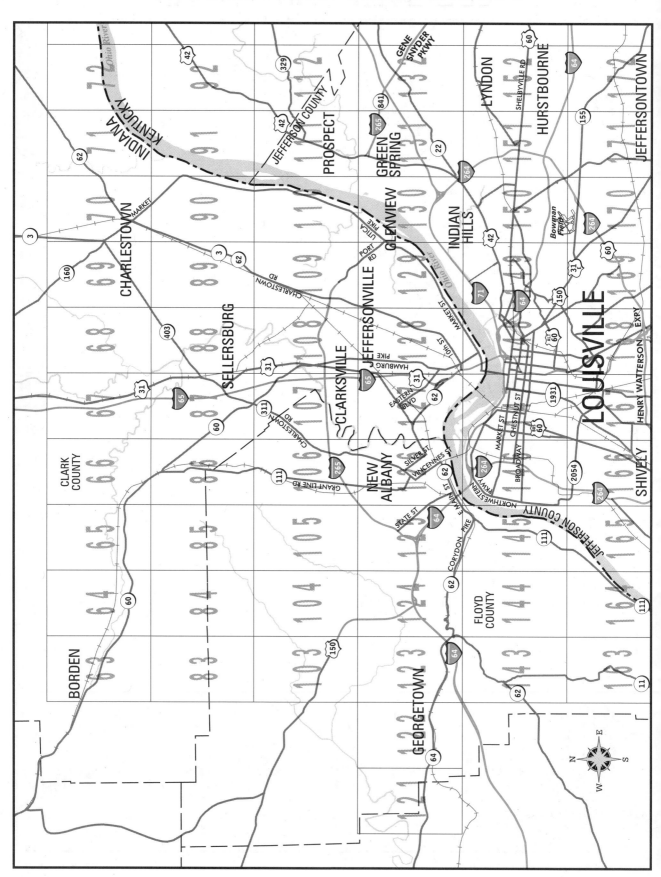

SCALE 1 Inch = 3 Miles

SOUTHWEST AREA COMPOSITE MAP

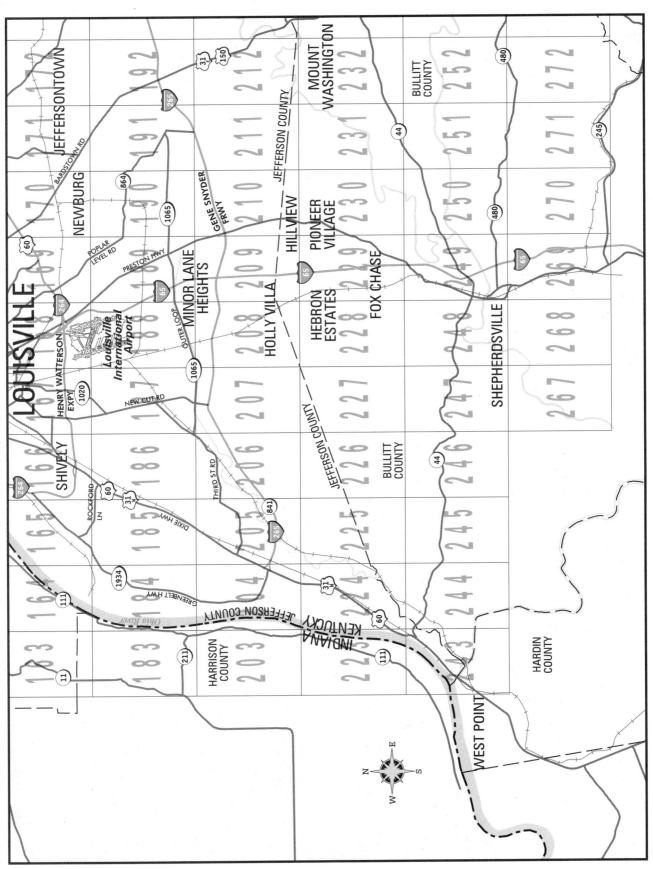

SCALE: 1 Inch = 3 Miles

NORTHEAST AREA COMPOSITE MAP

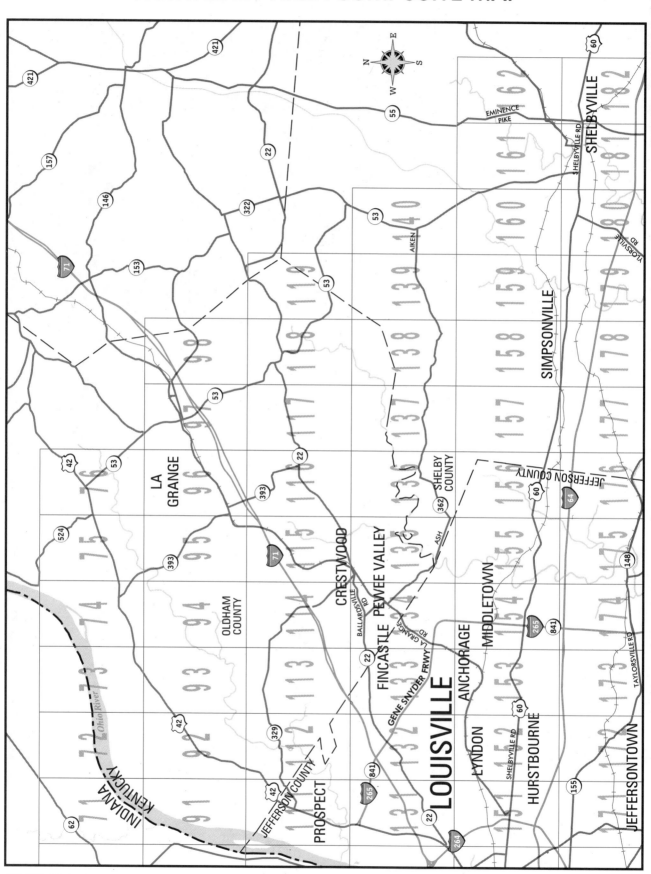

SCALE: 1 Inch = 3 Miles

SOUTHEAST AREA COMPOSITE MAP

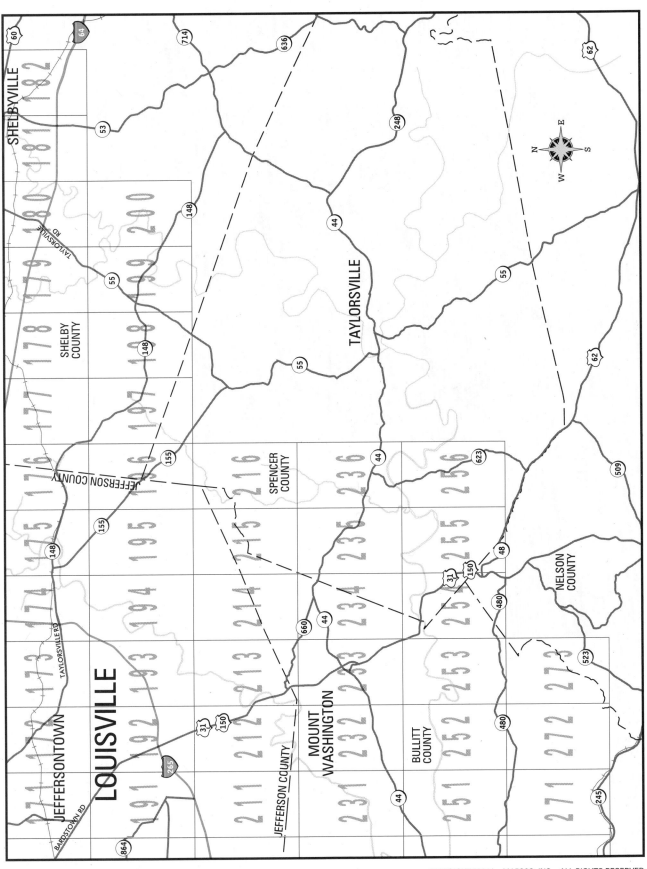

SCALE: 1 Inch = 3 Miles

NORTHWEST LOUISVILLE ZIP CODE BOUNDARIES

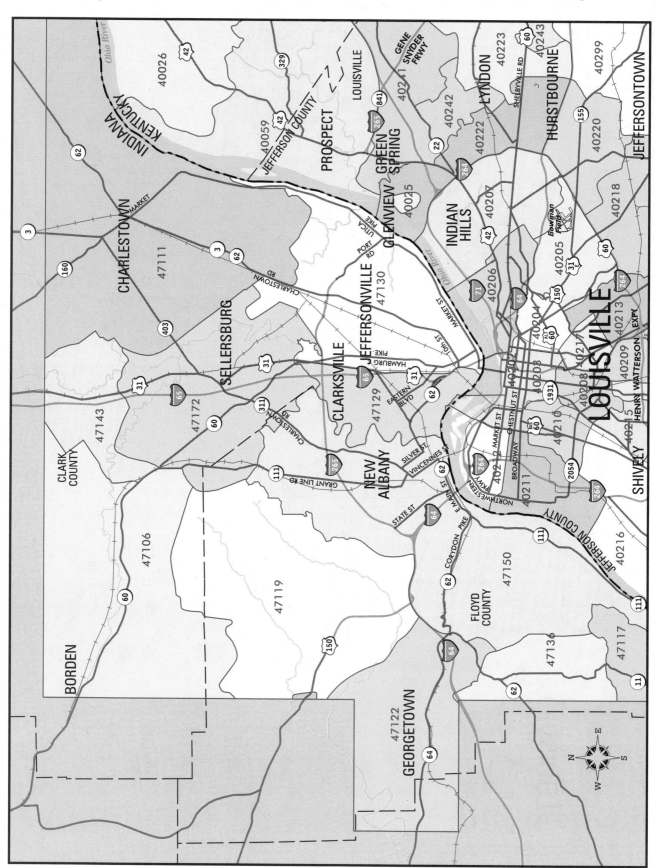

SCALE 1 Inch = 3 Miles

SOUTHWEST LOUISVILLE ZIP CODE BOUNDARIES

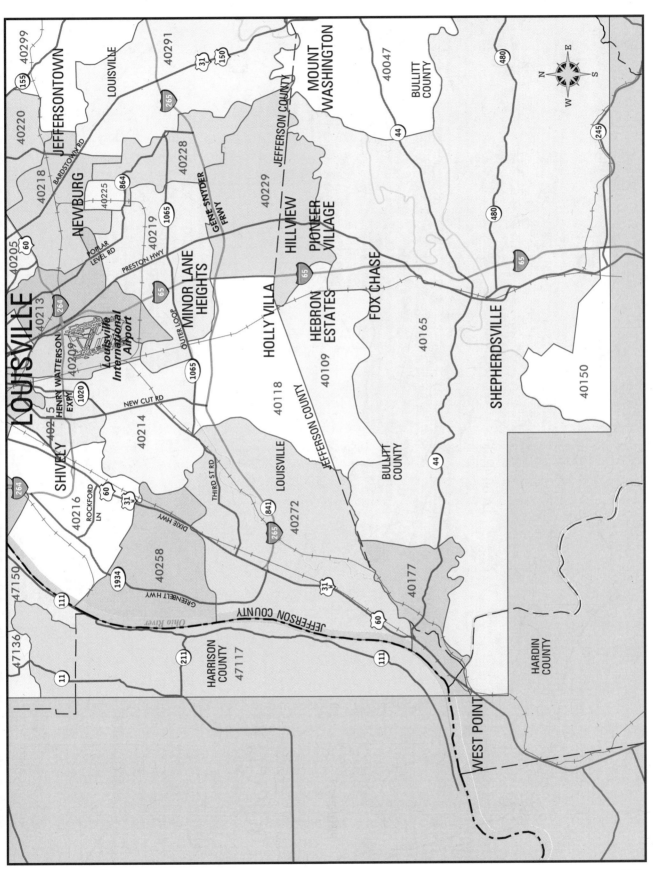

NORTHEAST LOUISVILLE ZIP CODE BOUNDARIES

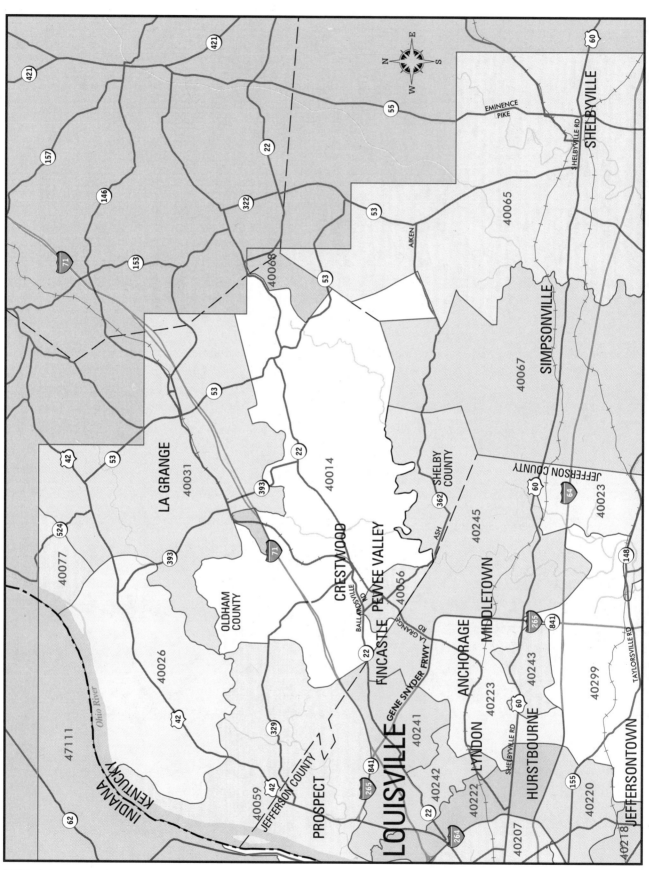

SCALE: 1 Inch = 3 Miles

SOUTHEAST LOUISVILLE ZIP CODE BOUNDARIES

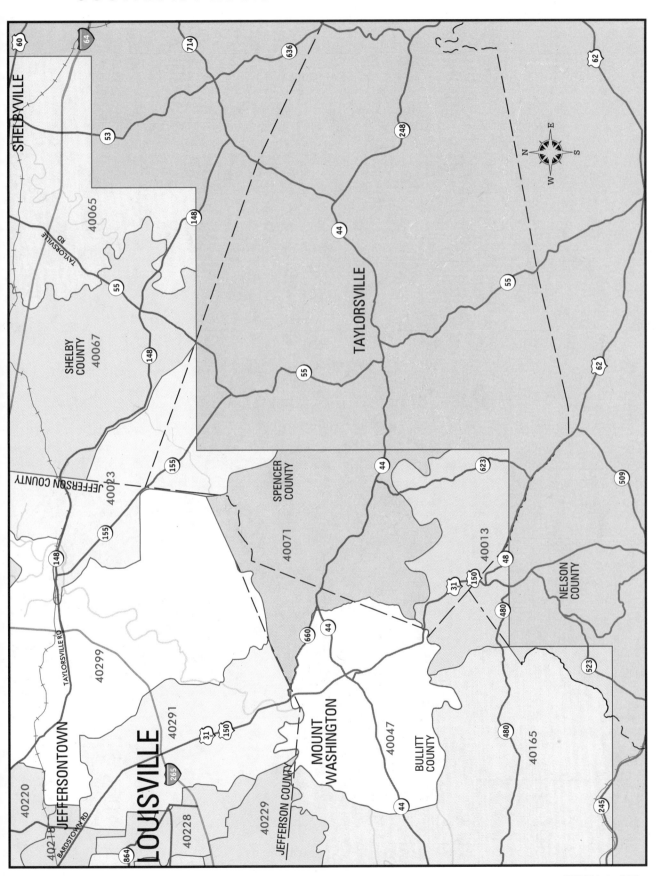

SCALE 1 Inch = 3 Miles

NORTHWEST LOUISVILLE SCHOOL DISTRICTS

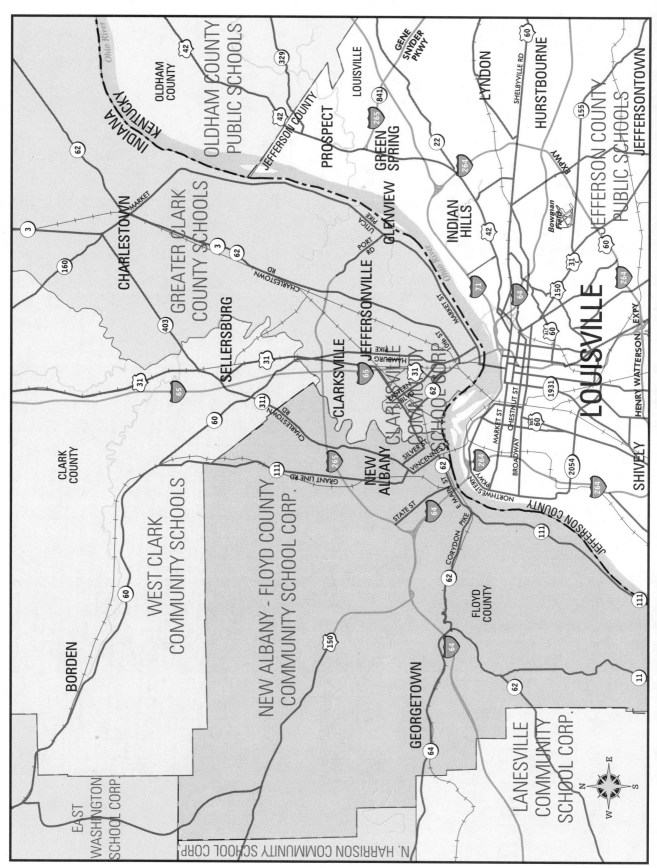

SCALE 1 Inch = 3 Miles

SOUTHWEST LOUISVILLE SCHOOL DISTRICTS

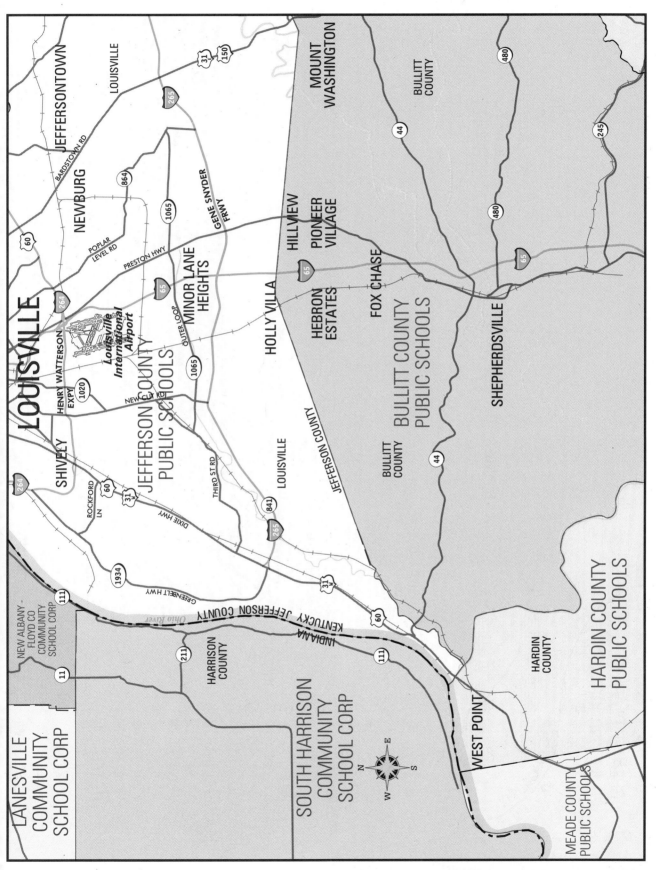

SCALE: 1 Inch = 3 Miles

NORTHEAST LOUISVILLE SCHOOL DISTRICTS

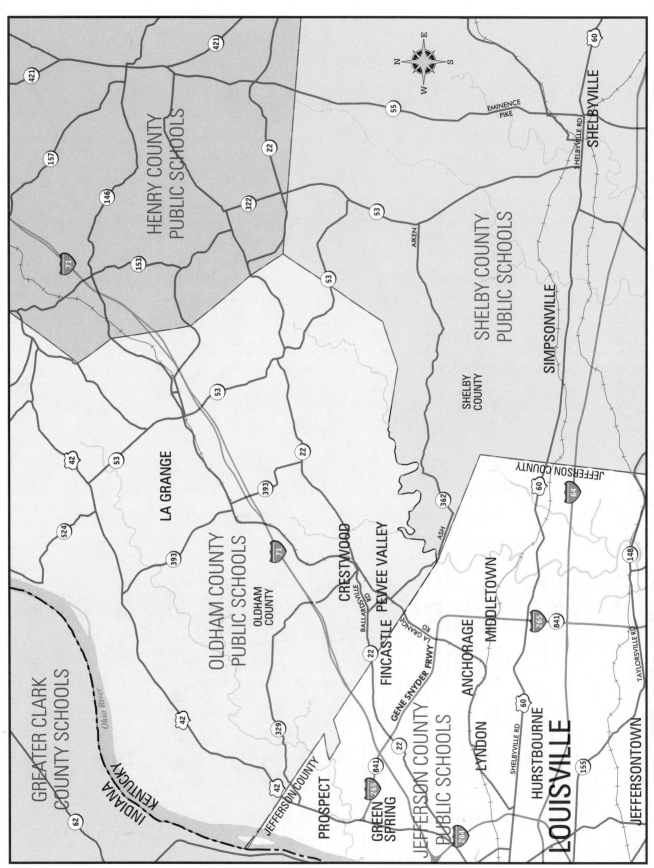

SCALE: 1 Inch = 3 Miles

SOUTHEAST LOUISVILLE SCHOOL DISTRICTS

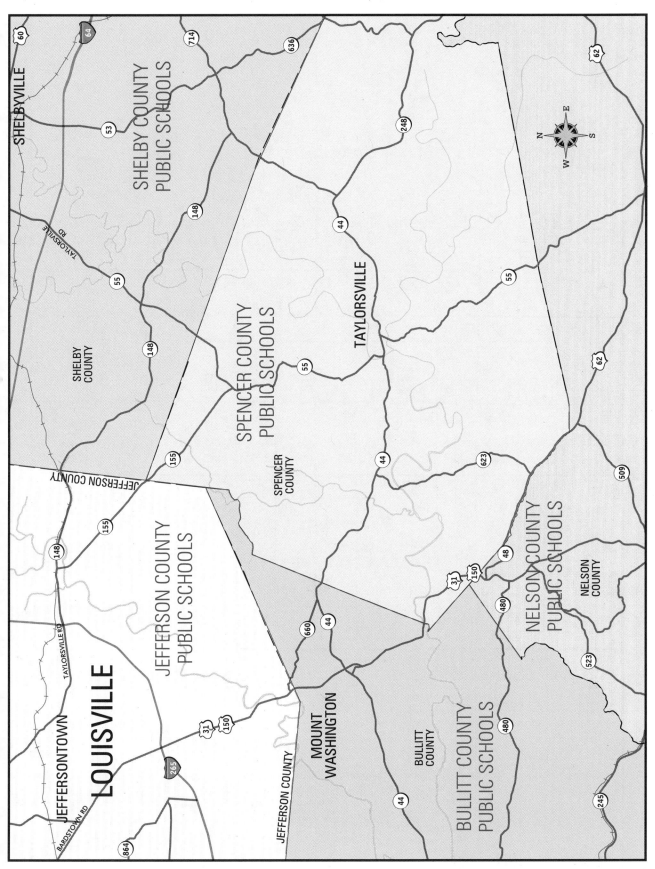

SCALE: 1 Inch = 3 Miles

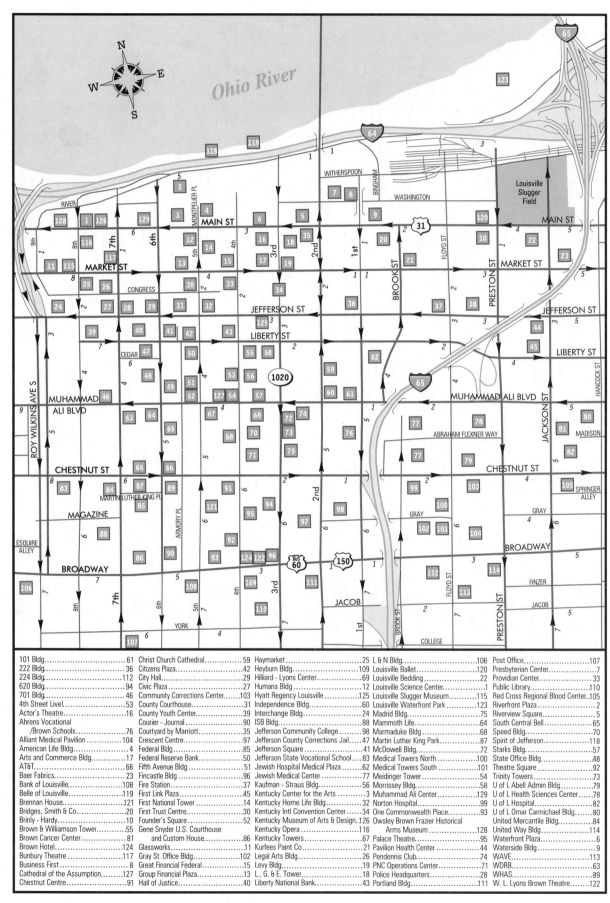

SCALE 1 Inch = 1100 Feet

LOUISVILLE INTERNATIONAL AIRPORT

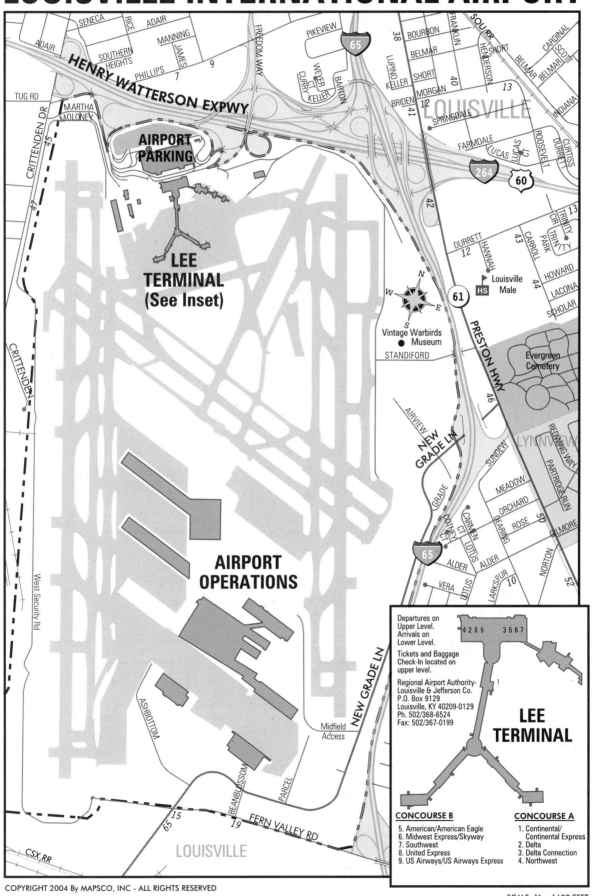

AIRPORT PARKING

LEE TERMINAL (See Inset)

AIRPORT OPERATIONS

HENRY WATTERSON EXPWY

Louisville Male

Vintage Warbirds Museum

Evergreen Cemetery

STANDIFORD

PRESTON HWY

NEW GRADE LN

West Security Rd

Midfield Access

FERN VALLEY RD

LOUISVILLE

CSX RR

LEE TERMINAL

Departures on Upper Level. Arrivals on Lower Level.

Tickets and Baggage Check-In located on upper level.

Regional Airport Authority-Louisville & Jefferson Co.
P.O. Box 9129
Louisville, KY 40209-0129
Ph. 502/368-6524
Fax: 502/367-0199

4 2 8 9   3 5 6 7

CONCOURSE B
5. American/American Eagle
6. Midwest Express/Skyway
7. Southwest
8. United Express
9. US Airways/US Airways Express

CONCOURSE A
1. Continental/Continental Express
2. Delta
3. Delta Connection
4. Northwest

SCALE: 1" = 1680 FEET

STREET NAME	CITY or COUNTY	MAP GRID	ZIP CODE	BLOCK RANGE	O/E
WESTWEGO PL	Louisville	172Y	40299	10100-10299	
WESTWIND RD	Indian Hills	130W	40207	100-299	
WESTWIND WAY	Oldham Co	114V	40014	6500-6599	
WESTWOOD AVE	Louisville	151X	40220	2400-2499	
WESTWOOD CT	Bullitt Co	210Y	40229	None	
WESTWOOD DR	Clark Co	88R	47111	6400-6699	
WESTWOOD DR	New Albany	125T	47150	1100-1299	
WESTWOOD DR	Oldham Co	115V	40014	4300-4499	
WESTWOOD DR	Woodland Hills	153U	40243	200-599	
WESTWOOD FARMS CT	Louisville	171Q	40220	7700-7799	
WESTWOOD FARMS DR	Louisville	171Q	40220	3400-3599	
WETHE CT	Louisville	192G	40291	5400-5499	
WETHERBY AVE	Middletown	153P	40243	11600-11999	
WETSTEIN AVE	Louisville	169D	40205	2300-2399	
WETTERAU AVE	Louisville	168B	40217	1000-1299	
WEWOKA AVE	Louisville	146B	40212	3800-4099	
WEXFORD DR	Louisville	170N	40218	3500-3599	
WEYANOKE CT	Prospect	111V	40059	8000-8099	
WEYBRIDGE GARDENS	St.Matthews	151J	40207	4700-4799	
WEYER CT	Louisville	168T	40209	4000-4099	
WEYLER AVE	Louisville	167J	40215	1200-1499	
WEYMOUTH CT	St.Matthews	151F	40222	1000-1099	
WHARTON CT	Louisville	191M	40291	8700-8799	
WHEATLEY CT	Newburg	170W	40218	4900-4999	
WHEATMORE DR	Louisville	166V	40215	3700E-3799E	
	Louisville	166V	40215	3700W-3799W	
WHEELER LN	Bullitt Co	232K	40047	100-999	
WHEELER AVE	Louisville	167S	40215	3500-3899	
	Louisville	167W	40215	3900-4299	
WHEELER RD	Floyd Co	144A	47150	None	
WHELAN LN	Jeffersonville	128T	47130	900-1299	
WHETSTONE WAY	Jeffersontown	152Y	40223	900-1199	
WHIPPANY CT	Louisville	184R	40258	6700-6899	
WHIPPERWILL RD	Louisville	186U	40214	7800-7899	
WHIPPLE RD	Louisville	224B	40272	680-7299	
WHIPPOORWILL DR	Louisville	209G	40229	9000-9099	
WHIPPOORWILL DR	Jeffersonville	129S	47130	1900-1999	
WHIPPOORWILL RD	Louisville	168M	40213	1600-3599	
WHIPPOORWILL HEIGHTS DR					
	Floyd Co	105Y	47150	300-399	
WHIPPORWILL DR	Norwood	151L	40222	200-299	
WHIPPS BEND DR	Bellemeade	152J	40222	8600-8699	
WHIPPS MILL RD	Louisville	151R	40222	8400-8899	
	Louisville	152F	40242	9000-9199	
	Bellemeade	152J	40222	8600-8799	
	Hurstbourne	151R	40222	100-199	
	Lyndon	151R	40222	8200-8399	
	Lyndon	152F	40242	9200-9699	
	Lyndon	152D	40223	9700-10499	
WHIRLAWAY CIR	Bullitt Co	233M	40047	100-299	
WHIRLAWAY CIR	Oldham Co	93A	40026	2800-2899	
WHIRLAWAY DR	Lyndon	152B	40242	1300-1399	
WHISP BROOK CIR	Louisville	209K	40229	100-399	
WHISPERING BROOK DR	Louisville	209K	40229	100-399	
WHISPERING HILLS BLVD	Louisville	190R	40219	5400-6199	
WHISPERING LEAF	Clark Co	107A	47172	6900-6999	
WHISPERING OAK DR	Louisville	209X	40118	None	
WHISPERING OAKS DR	Clark Co	88R	47111	6400-6599	
WHISPERWOOD CT	Oldham Co	92Y	40059	2100-2199	
WHISPERWOOD DR	Oldham Co	92Y	40059	2200-2299	
WHISPERWOOD TRAIL	Louisville	154M	40245	None	
WHITCOMB AVE	Clarksville	127Q	47129	400-699	
WHITE ASH CT	Louisville	210S	40229	4800-4899	
WHITE BLOSSOM BLVD	Louisville	132L	40241	9600-9999	
	Louisville	132Q	40241	9600-9999	
WHITE BLOSSOM CIR	Floyd Co	107K	47150	3100-3199	
WHITE BLOSSOM DR	Shepherdsville	268C	40165	100-299	
WHITEBLOSSOM ESTATES CT					
	Louisville	132Q	40241	3900-4099	
WHITEBLOSSOM ESTATES PL					
	Louisville	132Q	40241	9500-9599	
WHITE CEDAR DR	Louisville	190T	40219	8000-8099	
WHITE CEDAR PL	Louisville	190T	40219	7900-7999	
WHITE CLOVER WAY	Oldham Co	96L	40031	1000-1199	
WHITEGATE CT	Hurstbourne	152X	40222	9200-9299	
WHITEHALL CT	Louisville	206J	40272	3600-3799	
WHITE HAWK DR	Shelbyville	181U	40065	100-299	
WHITEHEATH CT	Douglass Hills	152V	40243	600-699	
WHITEHEATH LN	Douglass Hills	152V	40243	400-499	
WHITEHORSE VALE LN	Jeffersonville	128K	47130	1200-2699	
WHITEHOUSE DR	Louisville	192F	40291	9800-9899	
WHITEHOUSE DR	Oldham Co	116Y	40014	5600-5699	
WHITE OAK CT	Shelbyville	160Z	40065	1700-1799	
WHITE OAK DR	Bullitt Co	233R	40047	100-399	
WHITE OAK DR	Oldham Co	116B	40031	3200-3299	
WHITE OAK LN	Louisville	185M	40258	1900-2099	
WHITE OAK RD	Shelbyville	160Z	40065	100-199	
WHITE PINE DR	Louisville	189W	40219	None	
WHITE PINE WAY	Louisville	132M	40241	4400-4499	
WHITEPINE VIEW PL	Louisville	172V	40299	10500-10599	
WHITE PLAINS CT	Louisville	170M	40218	4000-4099	
WHITE PLAINS RD	Louisville	170M	40218	2900-2999	
WHITE POST WAY	Louisville	171F	40220	7500-7699	
WHITES LN	Louisville	207K	40118	700-999	
WHITE SPRUCE CT	Louisville	210S	40229	4900-4999	
WHITE SPRUCE DR	Louisville	210S	40229	11201-11299	O
WHITEWAY AVE	Louisville	169H	40205	2800-3099	
WHITEWOOD AVE	Louisville	168S	40209	4100-4399	
WHITEWOOD RIDGE DR	Louisville	156H	40245	None	
WHITFIELD DR	Louisville	171Y	40218	4800-7799	
WHITFIELD LN	Spencer Co	215T	40071	1-2099	
WHITLAND CT	Woodland Hills	153Q	40243	200-299	
WHITLEY RD	Louisville	206H	40272	9300-9399	
WHITLOCK ST	Louisville	189J	40213	2800-2899	
WHITLOW CT	Louisville	188H	40213	4500-4599	
WHITMORE AVE	Louisville	167W	40215	4300-4399	
	Louisville	187A	40215	4400-4799	
WHITNER CT	Sellersburg	87Z	47172	600-699	
WHITNEY CT	Bullitt Co	249A	40165	None	
WHITNEY AVE	Louisville	167T	40214	100E-299E	
	Louisville	167T	40214	100W-499W	
	Louisville	167T	40215	500W-1199W	
WHITNEY HILL CT	Louisville	173X	40299	4500-4599	
WHITNEY HILL RD	Louisville	173X	40299	11400-11499	
WHITNEY YOUNG	Shelby Co	177C	40067	None	
	Simpsonville	157Y	40067	None	
WHITSETT WAY	Charlestown	70E	47111	200-299	
WHITTAKER RD	Oldham Co	117T	40014	1600-1699	
WHITTIER AVE	Strathmoor Village	169D	40205	2600-2699	
WHITTIER DR	Clark Co	127F	47129	1700-1799	

STREET NAME	CITY or COUNTY	MAP GRID	ZIP CODE	BLOCK RANGE	O/E
WHITTINGHILL RD	Clark Co	68C	47143	2800-3699	
WHITTINGTON PKWY	Hurstbourne	152P	40222	100-399	
WHODA-THOT-IT HILL RD	Shelbyville	181C	40065	None	
WIBBEN AVE	Louisville	169C	40205	2200-2399	
WIBBLES HILL RD	Louisville	174D	40233	14700-14799	
	Louisville	174D	40233	14800-14999	
WICKER CT	Louisville	173X	40299	11700-11799	
WICKFIELD CT	Louisville	154U	40245	400-599	
WICKFIELD DR	Louisville	154U	40245	100-499	
WICKHAM WAY	Louisville	152B	40223	1700-1799	
	Whipps Millgate	152B	40223	1800-1999	
WICKLAND CT	Louisville	169L	40205	1800-1899	
WICKLAND RD	Louisville	169L	40205	3000-3099	
WICKLOW RD	Windy Hills	150D	40207	700-799	
WICKSBURY PL	Louisville	150T	40207	900-999	
WICTOR CT	Louisville	171G	40220	7700-7799	
WIDE SPRING CT	Coldstream	133G	40245	11900-12099	
WIDGEON AVE	Audubon Park	168L	40213	3100-3199	
WIEGLEIB AVE	Louisville	152M	40223	10100-10299	
WIESEKA RD	Clark Co	85Q	47119	4800-7099	
WIESEKA HILL RD	Clark Co	85J	47119	4800-7099	
WIGWAM RD	Indian Hills	150A	40207	None	
WILART DR	Louisville	166H	40210	1700-1799	
WILBURLOOK LN	Jeffersontown	172J	40220	2600-2699	
WILCHAR BLVD	Mount Washington	233J	40047	None	
WILD WAY	Hillview	209Y	40229	100-399	
WILDBRIAR CT	Oldham Co	116D	40031	1800-2099	
	Oldham Co	117A	40031	None	
WILDCAT DR	Louisville	206Q	40272	6800-6899	
WILDERNESS PL	Louisville	187K	40214	5400-5499	
WILDERNESS RD	Louisville	187K	40214	500-699	
WILDERNESS RD	Bullitt Co	228H	40109	100-899	
WILDERNESS TRAIL	Louisville	174U	40299	3400-3999	
WILDFLOWER TRAIL	Louisville	175L	40023	2200-2299	
WILDFLOWER WOODS CT					
	Jeffersontown	172Y	40299	10600-10699	
WILD FOX LN	Prospect	111V	40059	6700-6799	
WILD HORSE CT	Louisville	210K	40229	5400-5499	
WILD OAK CT	Lyndon	151L	40222	500-599	
WILDON CT	Jeffersontown	171M	40218	None	
WILDON PL	Jeffersontown	171M	40220	8700-8799	
WILD RIVER CT	Louisville	210K	40229	None	
WILD TURKEY DR	Oldham Co	117W	40014	3100-3199	
WILDWOOD CIR	Louisville	171X	40218	7000-7099	
WILDWOOD CT	Wildwood	152Q	40223	9800-9899	
WILDWOOD DR	Louisville	189W	40219	None	
WILDWOOD DR	Clark Co	127P	47129	2600-2799	
WILDWOOD LN	Louisville	206C	40272	9100-9999	
WILDWOOD LN	New Albany	125P	47150	900-1099	
WILDWOOD LN	Wildwood	152Q	40223	100-299	
WILDWOOD PL	Louisville	149Q	40206	300-399	
WILDWOOD RD	Clark Co	129K	47130	1-99	
WILDWOOD ST	Sellersburg	87Z	47172	500-699	
WILDWOOD TRAIL	Bullitt Co	232C	40047	100-799	
WILHELMINA AVE	Charlestown	70N	47111	None	
WILKE FARM AVE	Louisville	185E	40216	None	
WILKEN WAY	Louisville	224F	40272	13500-13599	
WILKERSON AVE	Louisville	185C	40216	2500-2599	
WILKERSON DR	Bullitt Co	232B	40047	100-899	
WILKIE RD	Louisville	185B	40216	2900-3299	
WILKINSON WOODS	Clark Co	84C	47106	None	
WILLAKATHA	Oldham Co	119F	40068	None	
WILLARD AVE	New Albany	126L	47150	2100-2399	
WILLENHALL CT	Douglass Hills	152V	40243	400-499	
WILLETT PL	Oldham Co	134C	40014	6900-6999	
WILLIAM ST	Louisville	148M	40206	100-199	
WILLIAM BECKETT DR	Louisville	166C	40211	None	
WILLIAM CLARK DR	Louisville	210D	40228	6700-6799	
WILLIAM CUMMINS CT	Louisville	191W	40228	8500-8599	
WILLIAM E. SUMMERS III AVE					
	Louisville	146X	40211	None	
WILLIAM E. SUMMERS III CT					
	Louisville	146X	40211	None	
WILLIAM PENN CT	Louisville	210D	40228	8800-8899	
WILLIAM PENN WAY	Louisville	210D	40228	8800-8999	
WILLIAMS CIR	Bullitt Co	231W	40165	None	
WILLIAMS DR	Clarksville	127U	47129	100-299	
WILLIAMS LN	Bullitt Co	214U	40071	100-599	
WILLIAMS LN	New Albany	145B	47150	2300-2599	
WILLIAMS RD	Louisville	215D	40299	8500-8799	
	Bullitt Co	215D	40299	8800-8999	
WILLIAMS ST	Jeffersonville	128N	47130	100-499	
WILLIAMSBOROUGH LN	Louisville	192K	40291	9500-9999	
WILLIAMSBURG CT	St.Matthews	150U	40207	1000-1099	
WILLIAMSBURG DR	Shelbyville	181D	40065	None	
WILLIAMSBURG PLAZA	Louisville	152T	40222	9500-9599	
WILLIAMSON CT	Louisville	154A	40223	1800-1999	
WILLIAMS RIDGE RD	Middletown	153X	40243	1200-1299	
WILLIAM VANCE CT	New Albany	125V	47150	1-99	
WILLINGER LN	Jeffersonville	128N	47130	100-299	
WILLIS	Shelbyville	181F	40065	None	
WILLIS AVE	Louisville	150P	40207	3700-3899	
	St.Matthews	150P	40207	3300-3699	
WILLIS DR	Louisville	207Q	40118	200-299	
WILLISMORE DR	Louisville	204R	40272	6200-6299	
WILLMAR AVE	Louisville	170L	40218	3700-3899	
WILLOUGHBY CT	Louisville	155S	40245	200-299	
WILLOW AVE	Louisville	149S	40204	1100-1499	
WILLOW AVE	Jeffersontown	172Q	40299	3600-3899	
WILLOW CT	Jeffersontown	172Q	40299	3600-3699	
WILLOW DR	Louisville	169X	40213	1300-1399	
WILLOW DR	Clark Co	72A	47111	16200-16299	
WILLOW DR	Jeffersonville	128J	47130	1500-1599	
WILLOW DR	New Albany	126H	47150	1500-1599	
WILLOW LN	Louisville	209T	40118	None	
WILLOW LN	Anchorage	153K	40223	11400-11599	
WILLOW LN	Clark Co	129L	47130	1-99	
WILLOW ST	New Albany	126V	47150	2100-2199	
WILLOW ST	Shelbyville	181B	40065	1001-1199	O
WILLOW WAY	Louisville	170K	40218	3300-3399	
WILLOW BEND DR	Oldham Co	136C	40014	7400-7799	
WILLOWBROOK CIR	Jeffersontown	152U	40223	9800-10199	
WILLOWBROOK CT	Oldham Co	92U	40059	2400-2499	
WILLOW BROOK RD	Woodland Hills	153U	40243	300-699	
WILLOW CREEK CT	Oldham Co	112E	40059	12900-12999	
WILLOW CREEK CT	Shelby Co	136S	40245	1000-1099	
WILLOWCREEK DR	Louisville	209B	40219	8900-9199	
WILLOW CREEK LN	Shelby Co	136S	40245	900-999	
* WILLOWCREST CIR	Louisville	131T	40242	None	
WILLOW FOREST DR	Louisville	134J	40245	12900-13299	

STREET NAME	CITY or COUNTY	MAP GRID	ZIP CODE	BLOCK RANGE	O/E
WILLOW FOREST PL	Louisville	134J	40245	4700-4799	
WILLOW GATE CT	Prospect	112N	40059	7300-7399	
WILLOW GLEN RD	Louisville	173Y	40299	12600-12699	
WILLOW GREEN WAY	Louisville	192S	40291	7900-7999	
WILLOW GROVE CIR	Louisville	154L	40245	14200-14499	
WILLOW GROVE CT	Louisville	154L	40245	14100-14199	
WILLOW GROVE WAY	Louisville	154L	40245	14100-14199	
WILLOWHURST PL	Jeffersontown	152U	40223	500-699	
WILLOWICK CT	Louisville	205T	40272	11200-11299	
WILLOW LAKE DR	Louisville	153A	40223	10800-10899	
WILLOW OAK LN	La Grange	97F	40031	1100-1399	
WILLOW PARK CIR	Middletown	153Z	40243	None	
WILLOW PARK DR	Middletown	153Z	40243	None	
WILLOW REED DR	Louisville	174S	40299	13700-13799	
WILLOW REED PL	Louisville	174S	40299	4100-4199	
WILLOW REED RD	Oldham Co	97B	40031	2300-2399	
WILLOWRUN CT	Oldham Co	135N	40056	8600-8699	
WILLOWRUN LN	Oldham Co	135N	40056	6600-6699	
WILLOW SPRINGS DR	Lyndon	152E	40242	900-1199	
	Lyndon	152E	40242	8800-9199	
WILLOW STONE CT	Louisville	153N	40223	11300-11399	
WILLOW STONE WAY	Louisville	153N	40223	100-599	
WILLOW TREE LN	Middletown	153Z	40243	None	
WILLOWVIEW BLVD	Louisville	173S	40299	4100-4399	
	Louisville	172V	40299	3800-4199	
	Jeffersontown	172V	40299	3800-4399	
WILLOW WOOD	Shelbyville	181E	40065	None	
WILLOWWOOD CT	Jeffersontown	172P	40299	3600-3699	
WILLOW WOOD DR	Bullitt Co	233M	40047	100-299	
WILLOWWOOD WAY	Jeffersontown	172N	40299	9000-9799	
WILLS CT	Louisville	146Y	40211	1400-1499	
WILMA AVE	Bullitt Co	210X	40229	100-399	
	Hillview	210X	40229	100-399	
WILMINGTON AVE	St.Matthews	150P	40207	3300-3899	
WILMINGTON DR	Mount Washington	223J	40047	3900-3999	
WILMOTH AVE	Louisville	164V	40216	4000-4499	
WILSHIRE AVE	Louisville	164V	40216	4100-4499	
WILSHIRE BLVD	Louisville	187Z	40214	1-99	
	Louisville	187Z	40214	1E-99E	
	Louisville	187Z	40214	1W-99W	
WILSON AVE	Louisville	147X	40210	1100-2599	
	Louisville	146Z	40211	2600-3199	
WILSON AVE	Louisville	133H	40223	None	
WILSON CT	La Grange	97L	40031	1200-1299	
WILSON LN	Sellersburg	107M	47172	7000-7199	
WILSON RD	Hardin Co	243X	40121	23100-23799	
WILSON ST	Lyndon	152A	40242	8900-9299	
WILSON SWITCH RD	Clark Co	65V	47106	None	
WILTON DR	Louisville	207L	40118	9700-9899	
WILTONWOOD CT	Louisville	205W	40272	11700-11799	
WILTSHIRE AVE	St.Matthews	150K	40207	100-199	
WIMBLEDON CT	Floyd Co	103W	47150	None	
WIMBLETON CT	Louisville	170J	40004	100-199	
WIMBLEY CT	Louisville	132P	40241	9300-9399	
WIMBORNE WAY	Hurstbourne	152N	40222	8400-8799	
WIMPLETON PL	Louisville	150N	40206	600-699	
WIMPOLE CT	Louisville	171J	40218	2900-2999	
WIMPOLE RD	Louisville	171J	40218	4000-4199	
WIMSETT WAY	Louisville	192E	40291	8800-8999	
WIMSTOCK AVE	Louisville	224F	40272	7200-7599	
WINBOURNE AVE	Clarksville	147C	47129	200-299	
WINBURN DR	Jeffersonville	129S	47130	1900-1999	
WINCHESTER CT	Bullitt Co	231F	40165	100-199	
WINCHESTER DR	Clark Co	129K	47130	2900-2999	
WINCHESTER DR	Floyd Co	107E	47172	2700-2899	
WINCHESTER DR	Mount Washington	233J	40047	100-499	
WINCHESTER RD	Louisville	150T	40207	3300-3599	
	Broad Fields	150T	40207	3500-3799	
	Fairmeade	150T	40207	4400-4599	
	St.Matthews	150Q	40207	3800-4399	
WINCHESTER ACRES RD	Louisville	133V	40245	2800-3000	
WINDBORN CT	Louisville	208A	40118	100-199	
WINDBROOK CT	Louisville	171Q	40220	4000-4099	
WINDEMERE DR	Louisville	186Q	40214	7200-7399	
WINDEMERE RD	Clarksville	127L	47129	400-599	
WINDFALL TRACE	Jeffersontown	152Q	40223	9900-9999	
WINDGATE DR	Louisville	192V	40291	None	
WINDHAM PKWY	Prospect	111P	40059	6800-7199	
WINDHURST CT	Windy Hills	151E	40207	900-999	
WINDHURST RD	Windy Hills	151E	40207	6600-6899	
WINDHURST WAY	Shelby Co	180J	40065	None	
WINDING RD	Louisville	187L	40214	5400-5499	
WINDING WAY	Shelby Co	182H	40065	100-499	
WINDING BLUFF CT	Louisville	130Z	40207	6000-6099	
WINDING BLUFF TRACE	Louisville	130Z	40207	2000-2099	
WINDING CREEK CT	Louisville	154G	40245	14000-14099	
WINDING CREEK PL	Louisville	154G	40245	1200-1299	
WINDING CREEK RD	Oldham Co	115H	40014	4200-4299	
WINDING OAKS TRAIL	Middletown	153K	40223	None	
WINDING SPRING CIR	Coldstream	133G	40245	4900-5099	
WINDING SPRING CT	Coldstream	133G	40245	12100-12199	
WINDING SPRING PL	Coldstream	133G	40245	5000-5099	
WINDING STREAM DR	Louisville	204Z	40272	6200-6399	
WINDING STREAM WAY	Louisville	204Z	40272	None	
WINDING VIEW TRAIL	Louisville	175M	40023	16700-16899	
WINDING WOODS TRAIL					
	Mount Washington	232Z	40047	None	
WINDMILL LN	Clark Co	129A	47130	1200-1499	
WIND RIDGE CT	Louisville	131K	40241	6800-6899	
WINDROW CT	Jeffersontown	152U	40223	10200-10299	
WINDROW PL	Windy Hills	150H	40207	6100-6199	
WINDSONG CT	Floyd Co	122H	47122	None	
WINDSONG CT	Windy Hills	150H	40207	6000-6099	
WINDSONG PL	Windy Hills	150H	40207	900-999	
WINDSONG WAY	Windy Hills	150H	40207	1000-1199	
WINDSOR DR	Clark Co	87X	47172	8900-9099	
WINDSOR DR	Floyd Co	125C	47150	None	
WINDSOR DR	Jeffersonville	128Y	47130	1100-1199	
WINDSOR PL	Louisville	148Z	40204	1600-1899	
WINDSOR FOREST DR	Louisville	206C	40272	2200-2999	
WINDSOR LAKES CT	Louisville	186X	40214	8100-8199	
WINDSOR LAKES PKWY	Louisville	186X	40214	2900-3099	
WINDSOR PARK DR	Louisville	206C	40272	9200-9299	
WINDSOR VIEW DR	Louisville	206G	40272	8600-8799	
WINDWARD CT	Oldham Co	92X	40059	2600-2999	
WINDWARD PL	Windy Hills	150H	40207	4300-4399	
WINDWARD WAY	Louisville	170G	40220	3600-3699	
WINDWOOD CT	Louisville	189X	40219	8300-8499	
WINDY PL	Clark Co	109B	47130	5800-5899	
WINDY WAY	Windy Hills	151A	40207	2500-2599	

W

STREET NAME	CITY or COUNTY	MAP GRID	ZIP CODE	BLOCK RANGE O/E
WINDY CREEK WAY	Floyd Co	107A	47150	1900-1999
WINDY ELM CT	Louisville	186D	40214	5700-5799
WINDYGO CT	Windy Hills	151A	40207	6300-6399
WINDY HILL RD	Bullitt Co	230B	40165	100-499
WINDY HILLS	Floyd Co	106E	47150	None
WINDY HILLS DR	Oldham Co	115Z	40014	4300-4499
WINDY OAKS RD	Louisville	132M	40241	4200-4499
WINDY RIDGE RD	Bullitt Co	251X	40165	100-499
WINDY WILLOW CT	Louisville	133F	40241	11500-11599
WINDY WILLOW DR	Louisville	133B	40241	5100-5499
	Oldham Co	133B	40241	5500-5699
WINE CELLAR CT	Louisville	205D	40272	None
WINESAP WAY	Louisville	191X	40228	7500-7599
WINFIELD DR	New Albany	125L	47150	300-399
WINGATE RD	Woodlawn Park	151E	40207	4300-4399
WINGED FOOT CT	Louisville	152L	40223	9900-9999
WINGED FOOT CT	Jeffersonville	128F	47130	1800-1999
WINGED FOOT DR	Louisville	152K	40223	9800-9999
WINGFIELD AVE	Louisville	167A	40210	2000-2099
WINGFIELD CIR	Oldham Co	97W	40031	2000-2099
WINGFIELD CT	Louisville	166H	40216	2200-2299
WINGFIELD LN	Louisville	166C	40210	1800-2599
	Louisville	166C	40210	2600-2899
WINGFIELD LN	Louisville	192T	40291	9700-10399
WINIFREDE LN	Louisville	149E	40206	1-99
WINKLER AVE	Louisville	167G	40208	300-1099
WINN AVE	Louisville	167Q	40214	400-499
WINNER CIR	Oldham Co	118A	40031	3500-3599
WINNERS CIR	Lyndon	152E	40242	1100-1199
WINNING COLORS DR	Mount Washington	233H	40047	None
WINNLAND DR	Louisville	189X	40219	340-3599
WINNROSE WAY	Louisville	146S	40211	4100-4599
WINSFORD PL	Crossgate	113W	40222	1800-1899
WINSLOW CIR	Louisville	205N	40272	5500-5599
WINSLOW DR	Louisville	205N	40272	5300-5499
WINSTEAD DR	Louisville	184X	40258	7100-7599
WINSTEWART RD	Floyd Co	122Q	47122	8200-8499
WINSTON AVE	Louisville	169H	40205	1900-2199
	Louisville	169H	40205	2200-2345
	Louisville	169H	40205	2346-2399
WINSTON CT	Hillview	209Z	40229	12100-12199
WINTER AVE	Louisville	148U	40204	1300-1599
WINTER WAY	Louisville	224D	40272	3000-3199
WINTERBERRY CIR	Louisville	150E	40207	3500-3599
WINTERBOURNE PL	Lyndon	151H	40222	8300-8399
WINTERBRANCH WAY	Louisville	154M	40245	None
WINTER GARDEN CT	Louisville	171S	40218	4300-4499
WINTER GARDEN WAY	Oldham Co	115N	40014	None
WINTERGREEN CT	Briarwood	132W	40242	8600-8699
WINTERGREEN RD	Louisville	205E	40272	5400-5499
WINTERHAVEN CT	Oldham Co	92U	40059	2300-2399
WINTERHAVEN RD	Louisville	171L	40220	2800-3099
WINTER HILL CT	Louisville	171V	40299	8300-8399
WINTERLEAF DR	Louisville	150J	40207	3600-3699
WINTER PARK DR	Louisville	171S	40218	4200-4399
* WINTER SPRINGS CT	Middletown	153Y	40243	1200-1299
WINTHROP AVE	Charlestown	69R	47111	100-199
WINTHROP LN	Louisville	131S	40222	6400-6499
WINTON AVE	Louisville	149H	40206	200-399
WINWOOD CT	Floyd Co	104P	47119	4200-4299
WINYAN LN	Louisville	152L	40223	500-699
WIRTH AVE	Louisville	168K	40217	3000-3099
WIRTH ST	La Grange	97F	40031	1-99
WISDOM LN	Louisville	211Q	40229	8700-8899
WISE CT	Hillview	229C	40229	4300-4399
WISELAND WAY	Hillview	229D	40229	4400-4499
WISEMAN CT	Louisville	205W	40272	5300-5399
WISERTOWN RD	Louisville	186Z	40214	8400-8499
WISSMAN RD	Floyd Co	122X	47122	1000-1399
	Georgetown	122X	47122	None
WISTERIA AVE	Lyndon	151M	40222	400-499
WITAWANGA AVE	Lyndon	151H	40222	1200-1399
WITHERSPOON	Louisville	148J	40202	100-199
WITHERSPOON ST E	Louisville	148J	40202	200-899
WITLOW AVE	Louisville	133M	40223	None
WITTEN CT	Charlestown	70J	47111	1-99
WITTEN DR	Louisville	205B	40258	5200-5399
WITTEN DR	Clark Co	69U	47111	8100-8299
WIZARD AVE	Louisville	167P	40215	3300-3499
WOERNER ST	Clarksville	147D	47129	1200-1599
WOLFCREEK CT	Louisville	131G	40241	7800-7899
WOLFCREEK PKWY	Louisville	131G	40241	4500-4799
WOLF DEN CT	Floyd Co	107P	47150	3000-3099
WOLF DRIVE CT	Oldham Co	117E	40031	1800-1999
WOLFE AVE	Louisville	168Q	40213	1200-1299
WOLFES CEMETERY RD	Floyd Co	121V	47122	9400-9899
	Georgetown	121R	47122	9400-9499
	Harrison Co	121V	47122	None
WOLFE TRACE	New Albany	126J	47150	1-99
WOLF LAIR CT	Floyd Co	107Q	47150	3000-3099
WOLF LAKE BLVD	Floyd Co	107P	47150	3000-3099
WOLFORD DR	Floyd Co	104T	47119	4700-4799
WOLFORD RIDGE CT	Louisville	154Y	40245	700-799
WOLF PEN LN	Louisville	131D	40059	1-99
WOLF PEN BRANCH RD	Louisville	131A	40059	6700-6899
	Louisville	131C	40059	7100-7999
	Louisville	132B	40059	8000-8899
	Prospect	131A	40059	6900-7099
WOLFPEN GLEN CT	Louisville	131C	40059	7600-7699
WOLFPEN RIDGE CT	Louisville	131C	40059	7400-7499
WOLFPEN RIDGE DR	Louisville	131C	40059	7700-7799
WOLF PEN TRACE	Louisville	111Z	40059	5600-5699
WOLFPEN WOODS CT	Louisville	131C	40059	7400-7499
WOLFPEN WOODS DR	Louisville	131C	40059	5000-5399
WOLF RIDGE CT	Floyd Co	107P	47150	None
WOLF RIDGE DR	Floyd Co	107Q	47150	None
WOLF RIDGE RD	Louisville	131C	40059	5600-5699
WOLF RUN RD	Louisville	207Q	40118	500-799
WOLFSPRING CT	Louisville	131G	40241	7600-7699
WOLFSPRING DR	Louisville	131G	40241	4600-4699
	Green Spring	131G	40241	4400-4599
WOLFSPRING TRACE	Green Spring	131G	40241	7300-7499
WOLLE DR	Louisville	204H	40272	None
WOOD	Shelby Co	182W	40065	None
WOOD AVE	Jeffersonville	128X	47130	800-999
WOOD AVE	New Albany	126C	47150	2100-2199
WOOD DR	New Albany	126L	47150	2100-2199
WOOD RD	Louisville	184R	40258	6200-6999
WOOD RD	Bellemeade	151M	40222	100-199
	Lyndon	151M	40222	200-599
WOOD ST	Charlestown	70S	47111	100-499
WOODBARK LN	Louisville	192N	40291	6600-6699
WOODBINE AVE	Louisville	148W	40208	100-599
WOODBINE LN	New Albany	125L	47150	100-299
WOODBLUFF TRACE	Louisville	154Q	40245	14600-14699
WOODBOURNE AVE	Louisville	169C	40215	1800-2199
	Louisville	149Z	40205	2200-2599
WOODBOURNE DR	New Albany	126B	47150	100-199
	New Albany	126B	47150	800-1199
WOODBRIAR CIR	Louisville	131T	40241	7200-7299
WOODBRIAR CT	Louisville	131T	40241	2900-2999
WOODBRIAR PL	Louisville	131T	40241	7100-7199
WOOD BRIAR RD	Louisville	131T	40241	7100-7299
WOODBRIDGE HILL LN	Louisville	111L	40059	None
WOODBRIDGE MEADOWS CT	Louisville	209B	40219	8900-8999
WOOD BROOK CT	Louisville	209K	40229	100-199
WOODBURY DR	Louisville	189X	40219	7900-8099
WOODCHAT WAY	Louisville	205D	40272	9100-9199
WOODCHESTER WAY	Louisville	208B	40118	400-499
WOODCLEFT RD	Bellemeade	152J	40222	200-299
WOODCOCK CIR	Lynnview	169W	40213	4900-4999
WOODCREEK CT	La Grange	97F	40031	1500-1599
WOODCREEK CT	Lyndon	151L	40222	8000-8199
WOODCREEK DR	La Grange	97F	40031	1200-1699
WOODCREEK RD	Seneca Gardens	149Z	40205	2500-2599
WOOD CREEK WAY	Clark Co	109R	47130	2500-2699
WOODCREST DR	Louisville	189V	40219	7900-7999
WOODCROFT CT	Jeffersontown	152Z	40223	1100-1199
WOODCROSS PL	Louisville	210P	40229	5500-5599
WOODDALE DR	Louisville	205C	40272	8900-9299
WOOD DUCK CIR	Clark Co	129P	47130	200-299
WOOD DUCK PL	Clark Co	129N	47130	2400-2499
WOODED WAY	Louisville	189H	40219	3900-4399
WOODED WAY	Hillview	209Y	40229	100-299
WOODED WAY	Jeffersonville	129A	47130	3000-3399
WOODED BEND WAY	Louisville	134P	40245	4300-4399
WOODED BRANCH LN	Louisville	192M	40291	None
WOODED CROWN RD	Middletown	153V	40243	300-399
WOODED FALLS RD	Middletown	153V	40243	100-399
WOODED FOREST RD	Middletown	153V	40243	12900-12999
WOODED GLEN CT	Jeffersontown	171M	40220	8500-8599
WOODED GLEN RD	Jeffersontown	172E	40220	8600-9199
WOODED HOBBS TRAIL	Louisville	208N	40118	None
WOODED LAKE DR	Louisville	193E	40299	5500-5699
WOODED LAKE DR	Shelby Co	177A	40067	1000-1099
WOODED MEADOW CT	Louisville	131P	40241	3000-3099
WOODED MEADOW RD	Louisville	131T	40241	7000-7099
WOODED OAK CIR	Worthington Hills	133F	40245	4600-4899
WOODED SPRINGS CT	Louisville	134P	40223	None
WOODED TRAIL CT	Jeffersontown	171H	40220	8700-8799
WOODED VALLEY DR	Louisville	125G	47150	300-399
WOODED VIEW DR	Clark Co	65W	47106	700-799
WOODED VIEW DR	Floyd Co	122C	47122	3600-3799
WOODED VIEW RD	Harrison Co	223A	47117	9000SE-9699SE
WOODFERN DR	Louisville	191L	40291	7900-8199
WOODFIELD CIR	Shelbyville	182N	40065	1-399
WOODFIELD CT	Shelbyville	182N	40065	1-99
WOODFIELD DR	Floyd Co	124B	47119	4300-4399
WOODFIELD DR	New Albany	106X	47150	1000-1099
WOODFIELD RD	Hurstbourne Acres	172A	40220	1800-1999
WOODFILL WAY	Louisville	169F	40205	1800-1899
WOODFORD PL	Louisville	149Y	40205	2000-2399
WOODGATE CT	Shively	166U	40216	4100-4199
WOODGATE LN	Louisville	171J	40220	3900-4003
	Louisville	171J	40220	4004-4499
WOODGREEN CT	Louisville	166V	40215	3700-3799
WOODGROVE PL	Louisville	134V	40245	None
WOOD HAVEN RD	Louisville	190D	40228	6700-6899
	Louisville	190D	40291	7000-7299
WOODHAVEN PLACE CIR	Louisville	190H	40228	6000-6099
WOODHAVEN PLACE DR	Louisville	190D	40228	6800-6999
WOODHILL CT	Oldham Co	117J	40014	5000-5099
WOODHILL LN	Louisville	190N	40219	4900-5399
WOODHILL RD	Indian Hills	130W	40207	1-99
WOODHILL VALLEY RD	Louisville	131E	40241	7400-7499
WOOD HOLLOW RD	Louisville	210E	40229	9400-9599
WOODHURST CT	Hurstbourne	152X	40222	9200-9299
WOODINGTON PL	Louisville	133V	40223	None
WOODKNOLL RD	Louisville	152R	40223	10200-10399
WOODLAKE DR	Louisville	154R	40245	500-699
WOODLAKE DR	Bullitt Co	233N	40165	100-299
WOOD LAKE DR	La Grange	97N	40031	500-599
WOODLAKE TRACE	Louisville	154M	40245	14600-14699
WOODLAND AVE	Louisville	146Z	40210	2000-2599
WOODLAND AVE	Louisville	133H	40223	None
WOODLAND AVE	Clark Co	88R	47111	6500-6599
WOODLAND AVE	La Grange	97J	40031	600-799
WOODLAND CT	Jeffersonville	128M	47130	2000-2599
WOODLAND CT	Clark Co	69Q	47111	None
WOODLAND DR	Louisville	189W	40219	None
WOODLAND DR	Clark Co	69Q	47111	8400-8599
WOODLAND DR	New Albany	126S	47150	100-299
WOODLAND RD	Louisville	146Y	40211	2600-3199
WOODLAND RD	Louisville	164Z	40216	3300-3399
WOODLAND RD	Anchorage	153G	40223	11800-12099
WOODLAND RD	Bullitt Co	248G	40165	1-99
WOODLAND RD	Clark Co	129K	47130	1-99
WOODLAND RD	Clark Co	128M	47130	2100-2199
	Jeffersonville	128M	47130	2000-2599
WOODLAND RD	New Albany	125U	47150	1600-1899
WOODLAND HEIGHTS DR	Louisville	154L	40245	900-999
WOODLAND HILLS DR	Spencer Co	235K	40071	1-999
WOODLAND LAKES DR	La Grange	97G	40031	200-499
WOODLAND PASS	Mount Washington	232Z	40047	None
WOODLAND RIDGE CIR	La Grange	97G	40031	700-999
WOODLAND RIDGE CT	Louisville	154L	40245	1000-1099
WOODLAND RIDGE CT	La Grange	97G	40031	300-399
WOODLAND RIDGE DR	Louisville	154L	40245	14200-14399
WOODLAND TRACE	Clark Co	67E	47143	1200-1299
WOODLAWN AVE	Louisville	168W	40209	100E-299E
	Louisville	168W	40209	300E-699E
	Louisville	167Y	40214	100W-599W
	Louisville	167X	40215	600W-1299W
WOODLAWN AVE	Jeffersonville	128N	47130	100-399
WOODLAWN AVE	La Grange	97J	40031	100-199
WOODLAWN DR	New Albany	126L	47150	1600-1699
WOODLAWN RD	Shelby Co	182Y	40065	1-3799
WOODLEA LN	Louisville	149C	40207	1-99
WOODLEY WAY	Louisville	209M	40229	10100-10199
WOODLUCK AVE	Louisville	150Z	40205	1500-1699
WOODMERE AVE	Shively	166H	40216	2600-2799
WOODMONT DR	Louisville	151X	40220	2300-2699
	St.Regis Park	151X	40220	2700-2899
WOODMONT PARK LN	Louisville	134V	40245	3500-4299
WOODMONT PARK PL	Louisville	134V	40245	14800-14899
WOODMORE AVE	Louisville	187Q	40214	1-199
	Louisville	187L	40214	700-799
WOODMOUNT DR	New Albany	125T	47150	1000-1099
WOODPECKER CT	Louisville	185B	40216	3000-3099
WOODPOINTE BLVD	Louisville	209C	40219	8800-8899
WOODPOINTE CT	Bullitt Co	233N	40047	100-299
WOODREED CT	Orchard Grass Hills	133D	40014	9200-9299
WOODREED PL	Orchard Grass Hills	133D	40014	7400-7499
WOODRIDGE DR	Charlestown	69V	47111	100-299
WOODRIDGE DR	Pewee Valley	134K	40056	7600-7699
WOODRIDGE RD	Louisville	205S	40272	11400-11599
WOODRIDGE LAKE BLVD	Louisville	205S	40272	5200-5299
WOODRIDGE LAKE WAY	Louisville	205S	40272	11200-11299
WOOD ROCK RD	Louisville	191F	40291	7200-7399
WOODROSE CT	Prospect	111V	40059	8200-8299
WOODROW AVE	New Albany	126R	47150	300-699
WOODROW LN	Bullitt Co	270X	40165	100-299
WOODROW WAY	Louisville	190R	40228	6600-7299
WOODROW WAY	St.Matthews	150K	40207	None
WOODRUFF AVE	Louisville	167S	40215	3500-3899
	Louisville	167W	40215	3900-4099
WOODS LN	Bullitt Co	208Y	40109	100-399
WOODS BEND DR	Bullitt Co	228M	40109	200-499
WOODSBORO RD	Oldham Co	117J	40014	1800-1999
WOODS CLUB CT	Louisville	131T	40241	7000-7099
WOODS CLUB RD	Louisville	131T	40241	2800-2899
WOODSDALE AVE	Louisville	151W	40220	2600-2699
WOODSDALE RD	Bullitt Co	253X	40165	100-4299
	Bullitt Co	272V	40165	100-4299
WOODS EDGE	Clark Co	64Y	47106	None
WOODSEND RD	Louisville	210F	40229	4900-5099
WOODSIDE CT	Bullitt Co	233Q	40047	100-199
WOODSIDE DR	Louisville	130T	40207	2300-2799
WOODSIDE DR	Clark Co	127F	47129	None
WOODSIDE DR	New Albany	126C	47150	900-1099
WOODSIDE DR	Oldham Co	91Z	40059	12600-12699
WOODSIDE PL	Glenview	130K	40222	None
WOODSIDE RD	Glenview	130K	40222	3100-3699
WOODSIDE HILL RD	Glenview	130Q	40025	5100-5199
WOODSIDE POINTE CT	Louisville	130T	40207	5300-5399
WOODSMAN CT	Louisville	189X	40219	8300-8399
WOODSONG CT	Louisville	192M	40291	11300-11399
WOOD SPRINGS RD	La Grange	97N	40031	400-599
WOODSTOCK DR	Clarksville	127C	47129	900-999
WOODSTOCK RD	Blue Ridge Manor	152R	40223	10200-10299
WOODSTONE DR	Floyd Co	124L	47119	1-99
	Floyd Co	124L	47119	4000-4099
WOODSTONE WAY	Louisville	131E	40241	4000-4299
WOODSTREAM PL	Louisville	154M	40245	14600-14699
WOODSVIEW CT	Floyd Co	105K	47119	6000-6099
WOODS VIEW PL	Louisville	134P	40245	4100-4199
WOODTHRUSH TRAIL	Louisville	154H	40245	None
WOODTWIST CT	Louisville	192Z	40291	10800-10899
WOOD VAIL CT	Louisville	131J	40241	6500-6599
WOOD VALLEY CT	Bullitt Co	214R	40299	100-13899
WOOD VALLEY LN	Bullitt Co	214Q	40299	100-8899
WOODVIEW CIR	Middletown	153L	40243	500-599
WOODWARD DR	St.Regis Park	171C	40220	2800-2899
WOODWAY LN	Louisville	146S	40211	1000-1099
WOODWIND CT	Jeffersontown	152U	40223	9800-10099
WOODWIND CT	Mount Washington	232Z	40047	None
WOODWYND WAY	Jeffersontown	152Z	40223	1100-1199
WOODY AVE	Louisville	167W	40215	1400-1499
WOOLDRIDGE AVE	Pewee Valley	134C	40056	300-399
WOOLDRIDGE PL	Pewee Valley	134G	40056	100-199
WOOLRICH RD	Graymoor/Devondale	151B	40222	7100-7299
WORTH AVE	Pioneer Village	230E	40165	1300-1399
WORTH CT	Oldham Co	116L	40014	2600-2699
WORTH RD	Oldham Co	116L	40014	2600-2699
WORTHING CT	Louisville	154Q	40245	400-499
WORTHINGTON LN	Louisville	112Z	40059	10200-10599
	Oldham Co	113W	40059	10600-11299
WORTHINGTON WAY	Louisville	132D	40059	None
WORTHINGTON GLEN DR	Louisville	132D	40241	10100-10399
WORTHINGTON PLACE DR	Louisville	133E	40241	5400-5499
WREN RD	Audubon Park	168L	40213	3200-3399
WREN RD	Crestwood	134H	40014	6700-6799
WREN RD	New Albany	126F	47150	2000-2099
WROCKLAGE AVE	Louisville	169C	40205	1900-2399
WROUGHT IRON WAY	Floyd Co	123X	47122	6500-6599
WUNDERLY CT	Louisville	191P	40291	6800-6899
WURTELE AVE	Louisville	167F	40208	1400-1599
	Shively	166M	40216	2900-3099
WYANDOT CT	Shepherdsville	249K	40165	1-199
WYANDOTTE AVE	Louisville	166C	40210	2600-3099
WYCKFORD WAY	Louisville	170K	40218	2500-2599
WYCKOFF CT	Louisville	184R	40258	6700-6799
WYCKSHIRE CT	Clark Co	127B	47129	1900-1999
WYCLIFFE CT	Prospect	111J	40059	7500-7599
WYCLIFFE DR	Prospect	111J	40059	7400-7499
WYETH CT	Louisville	171F	40220	2500-2599
WYNBROOKE CIR	Louisville	132Q	40241	3100-3799
WYNBROOKE CIR	Louisville	132Q	40241	3700-3799
WYNBROOKE PL	Louisville	132U	40241	9900-9999
WYNCLIFF CT	Louisville	132Q	40241	9900-9999
WYNDEFAIR CT	Prospect	131B	40059	7200-7299
WYNDEMERE CT	Floyd Co	107F	47150	3500-3599
WYNDHAM PKWY	Prospect	111P	40059	6800-7199
* WYNDHAM WAY	Jeffersontown	172V	40299	3600-3799
WYNDINGBROOK LN	Bullitt Co	229U	40165	2300-2399
WYNDRIDGE CREEK WAY	Lyndon	152E	40222	None
WYNDSWEPT CT	Floyd Co	107F	47150	3400-3499
WYNFIELD CLOSE CT	Louisville	149G	40206	400-499
WYNFIELD MEWS LN	Louisville	149G	40206	3000-3099
WYNMEADE PL	Louisville	133U	40223	None
WYNNWOOD CIR	Northfield	131S	40222	2200-229
WYOLA CT	Louisville	170R	40218	4300-4399
WYTHE HILL CIR	Prospect	111Q	40059	6900-6999
WYTHE HILL PL	Prospect	111Q	40059	7100-7199

*See Detail Map Section on Page 81

W

STREET NAME	CITY or COUNTY	MAP GRID	ZIP CODE	BLOCK RANGE O/E
X				
No "X" Streets				
Y				
YAGER CT	Louisville	132M	40241	10500-10599
YAGER LN	Louisville	133J	40241	4500-4599
YAGER LN	La Grange	97K	40031	200-599
	La Grange	97K	40031	1000-1799
YAKIMA ST	Louisville	187N	40214	1100-1199
YALE DR	Louisville	169B	40205	1700-1999
YALE DR	Clarksville	127M	47129	700-799
YANCY LN	Maryhill Estates	150G	40207	600-699
YANDELL DR	Louisville	133U	40223	11300-11399
	Louisville	133T	40023	None
YANKEE LN	Louisville	190K	40219	5400-5499
YARDLEY CT	Louisville	171V	40299	3801-3999
YARMOUTH CT	Louisville	206F	40272	9600-9699
YARWOOD RD	Louisville	130M	40222	3800-389
YAUPON LN	Louisville	170W	40213	5000-5199
YEARLING DR	Bullitt Co	229N	40109	100-499
YELLOW WOOD CT	Lyndon	152E	40242	None
YELLOW WOOD PL	Lyndon	152E	40242	8900-8999
YELLOW PINE CT	Louisville	210H	40229	9500-9599
YELLOW PINE DR	Louisville	210H	40229	6100-6399
YELLOW SANDS DR	Louisville	190L	40219	6000-6199
YENOWINE LN	Floyd Co	123Z	47122	61-999
YE OLD POST RD	Louisville	190K	40219	5400-5499
YEW LN	Louisville	170W	40213	5000-5399
YOCUMSHIRE DR	Jeffersontown	172W	40299	4600-4699
YOLANDA DR	Louisville	166Y	40216	4400-4499
YORK ST	Louisville	147Q	40203	200-899
YORK RIVER RD	Louisville	187R	40214	7200-7399
YORKSHIRE BLVD	Louisville	171A	40220	2800-2999
YORKSHIRE BLVD	Bullitt Co	246K	40165	100-1399
YORKSHIRE DR	Shelbyville	161N	40065	1300-1399
YORKTOWN CT	Louisville	187V	40214	7300-7399
YORKTOWN RD	Louisville	187Z	40214	7100-7799
YORKTOWN TERRACE	Louisville	187U	40214	7100-7299
YORKWOOD PL	Jeffersontown	152U	40223	700-799
YOUNG AVE	Louisville	146X	40211	3000-3899
YOUNG CT	Louisville	146X	40211	1600-1699
YOUNG ST	New Albany	125Z	47150	700-799
YOUNGLAND AVE	Shively	166G	40216	1700-1999
YOUNGSTOWN CT	Louisville	205Q	40272	3100-3199
YOUNGSTOWN RD	Louisville	205Q	40272	10800-10999
YOUNGWOOD RD	Louisville	170P	40218	3700-3899
YUCCA LN	Louisville	185P	40258	5500-5599
YUMA WAY	Louisville	204G	40258	6800-7099
YVETTE CT	Louisville	191S	40228	7700-7799
YVONNE CT	Louisville	191S	40228	6800-6899
Z				
ZABEL WAY	Louisville	192A	40291	8700-8899
ZACHARY CIR	Louisville	187U	40214	8700-8799
ZACHARY DR	Oldham Co	98N	40031	1700-1899
ZALE SMITH RD	Oldham Co	97R	40031	1700-2699
ZANE ST	Louisville	147U	40203	500-799
	Louisville	147T	40210	1000-1299
ZARING MILL CIR	Louisville	132Q	40241	3800-3899
ZARING MILL CT	Louisville	132Q	40241	3900-3999
ZARING MILL RD	Shelby Co	181S	40065	700-6599
	Shelbyville	181N	40065	None
	Shelby Co	200H	40065	None
ZAYRE RD	Louisville	185H	40216	4100-4199
ZEPHYR CT	Louisville	171K	40220	7500-7599
ZELKOVA DR	Shelbyville	181A	40065	1-99
ZELMA PL	Bullitt Co	230H	40165	100-299
ZELMA FIELDS AVE	Louisville	191Y	40228	8000-8399
ZENA'S CT	Shelbyville	181V	40065	1-199
ZENITH WAY	Louisville	190U	40219	7700-7899
ZERMATT CT	Oldham Co	113X	40059	None
ZETA CT	Louisville	169S	40213	4500-4599
ZEUS CT	Louisville	185P	40258	6700-6799
ZEV WAY	Louisville	205E	40272	5400-5499
ZIB LN	Louisville	189W	40219	2600-2899
ZIEGLER AVE	Louisville	168A	40217	700-799
ZILMA DR	Louisville	165T	40216	4700-4799
ZINNA RD	Hillview	210X	40229	100-199
ZINNIA WAY	Bullitt Co	230H	40165	100-699
ZIX DR	Lyndon	152D	40223	10200-10299
ZOELLER AVE	Louisville	165R	40216	4100-4299
ZONETON RD	Bullitt Co	230F	40165	100-5199
	Bullitt Co	231K	40165	100-5199
ZORN AVE	Louisville	149G	40206	100-1399
ZORN PL	Louisville	149G	40206	1-99
ZORRA CT	Louisville	191G	40291	5600-5699
ZORRO PL	Bullitt Co	231E	40165	100-299
ZULAUF AVE	Jeffersonville	128Y	47130	500-599
ZURICH CT	Oldham Co	113X	40059	None
ZURSCHMEIDE DR	New Albany	125M	47150	2400-2499

Notes

Notes

Notes

Detail Map Section

Maps in the "Detail Map Section" are enlargements of selected areas within the Louisville MAPSCO's coverage which cannot be clearly shown on our regular maps due to the density of streets within these areas. To enable you to easily spot these high density areas of our regular maps, they have been highlighted in a grey tint with the following note:

SEE DETAIL MAP
SECTION ON
INDEX PAGE 81

If, in the regular course of using your MAPSCO, you cannot find the street required within the grid indicated by MAPSCO's index ... Please check the "Detail Map Section".

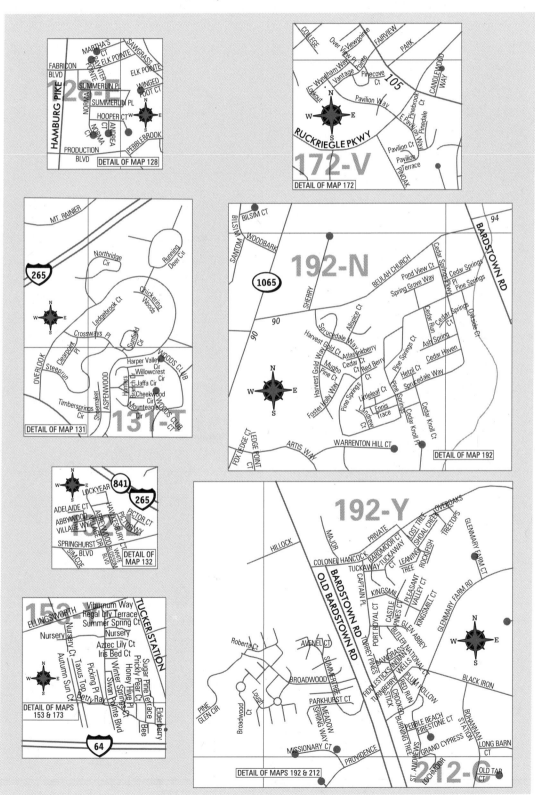

SCALE: 1" = 1000'

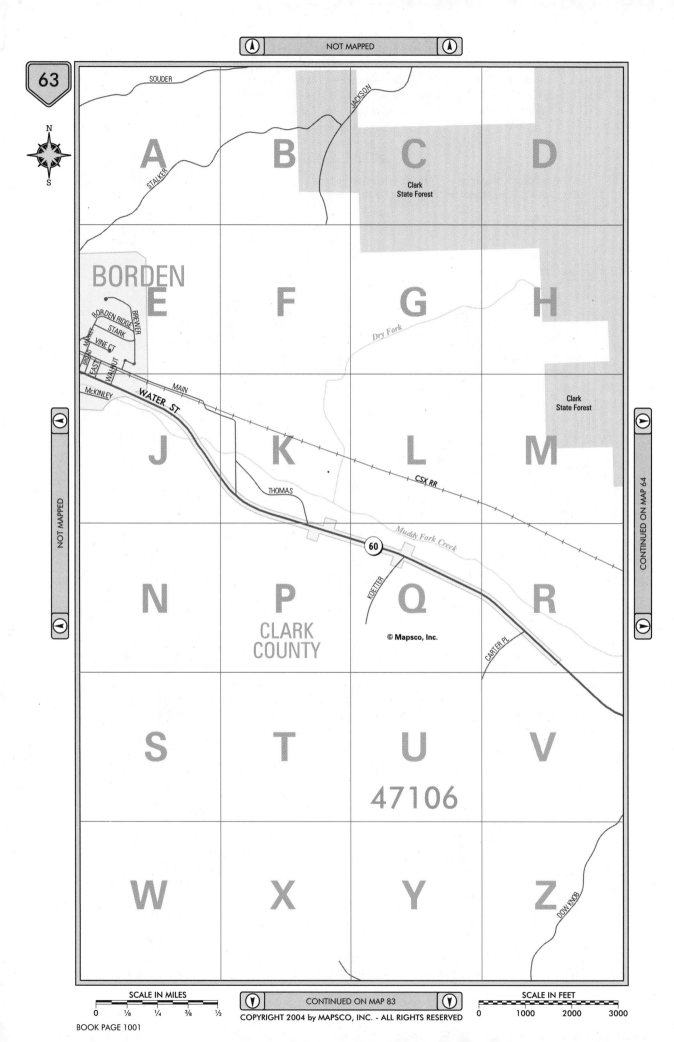

63

N
W E
S

A   B   C   D

Clark
State Forest

BORDEN

E   F   G   H

Dry Fork

BORDEN RIDGE
BREWER
STARK
MARKET
VINE CT
BROAD
EAST
WALNUT

SOUDER

STALKER

Clark
State Forest

McKINLEY   WATER ST   MAIN

J   K   L   M

CSX RR

THOMAS

NOT MAPPED

CONTINUED ON MAP 64

Muddy Fork Creek

60

KOETTER

© Mapsco, Inc.

N   P   Q   R

CLARK
COUNTY

CARTER PL

S   T   U   V

47106

W   X   Y   Z

DOW KNOB

SCALE IN MILES
0   1/8   1/4   3/8   1/2

CONTINUED ON MAP 83

SCALE IN FEET
0   1000   2000   3000

BOOK PAGE 1001

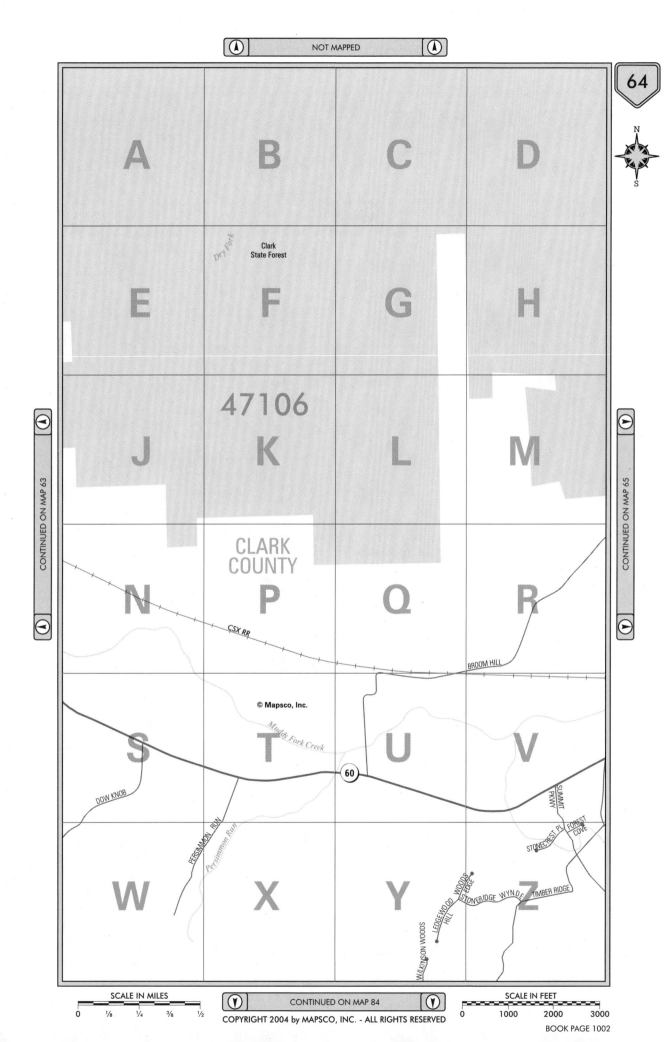

64

N
S

A B C D

E F G H

Clark
State Forest

Dry Fork

47106

J K L M

CONTINUED ON MAP 63

CONTINUED ON MAP 65

CLARK
COUNTY

N P Q R

CSX RR

BROOM HILL

© Mapsco, Inc.

Muddy Fork Creek

S T U V

60

DOW KNOB

PERSIMMON RUN

Persimmon Run

SUMMIT PRWY

STONECREST PL

FOREST COVE

W X Y Z

LEDGEWOOD WOODS

WILKINSON WOODS

STONERIDGE

HILL

ST RIDGE

WYNDE

TIMBER RIDGE

SCALE IN MILES

0   ⅛   ¼   ⅜   ½

CONTINUED ON MAP 84

SCALE IN FEET

0   1000   2000   3000

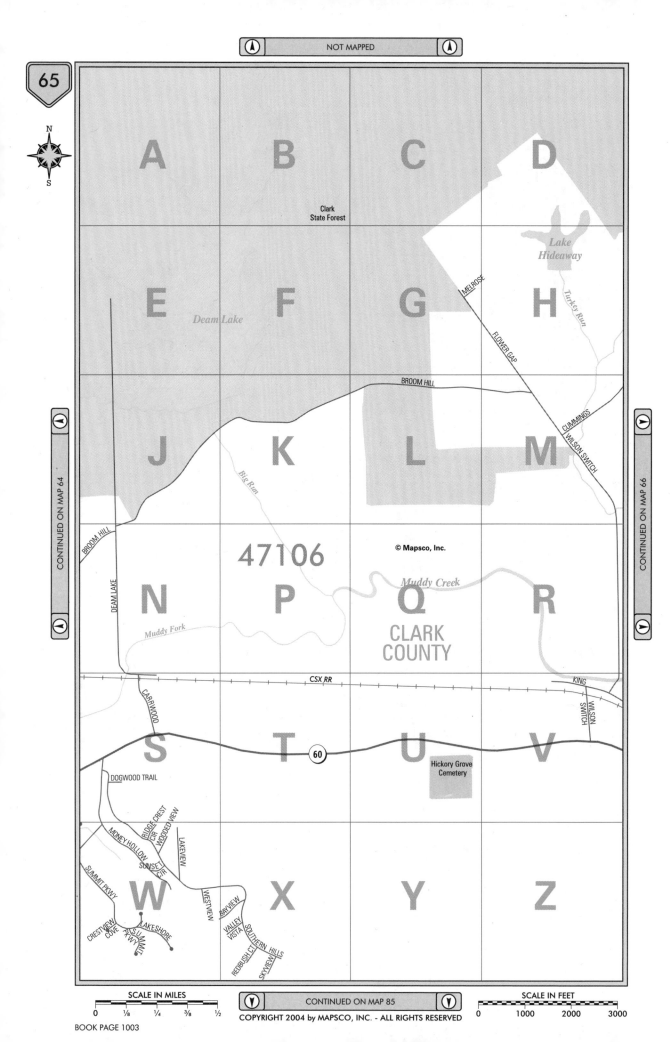

65

N
S

A

B

C

D

Clark
State Forest

Lake
Hideaway

E

F

G

Melrose

H

Dean Lake

Turkey Run

BROOM HILL

J

K

L

M

Flower Gap

Big Run

Cummings

Wilson Switch

CONTINUED ON MAP 64

CONTINUED ON MAP 66

BROOM HILL

DEAN LAKE

47106

© Mapsco, Inc.

Muddy Creek

N

P

Q

R

CLARK
COUNTY

Muddy Fork

CSX RR

KING

CARRWOOD

WILSON SWITCH

S

T

60

U

V

Hickory Grove
Cemetery

DOGWOOD TRAIL

BUDGE CREST CIR
MONEY HOLLOW
WOODED VIEW
LAKEVIEW
SUNSET CIR

W

X

Y

Z

SUMMIT PKWY
WESTVIEW
BAYVIEW
VALLEY VISTA
SOUTHERN HILLS

CRESTVIEW COVE
LAKESHORE
SUMMIT PKWY
REDBUSH CT
SKYVIEW

SCALE IN MILES
0   ⅛   ¼   ⅜   ½

CONTINUED ON MAP 85

SCALE IN FEET
0   1000   2000   3000

BOOK PAGE 1003

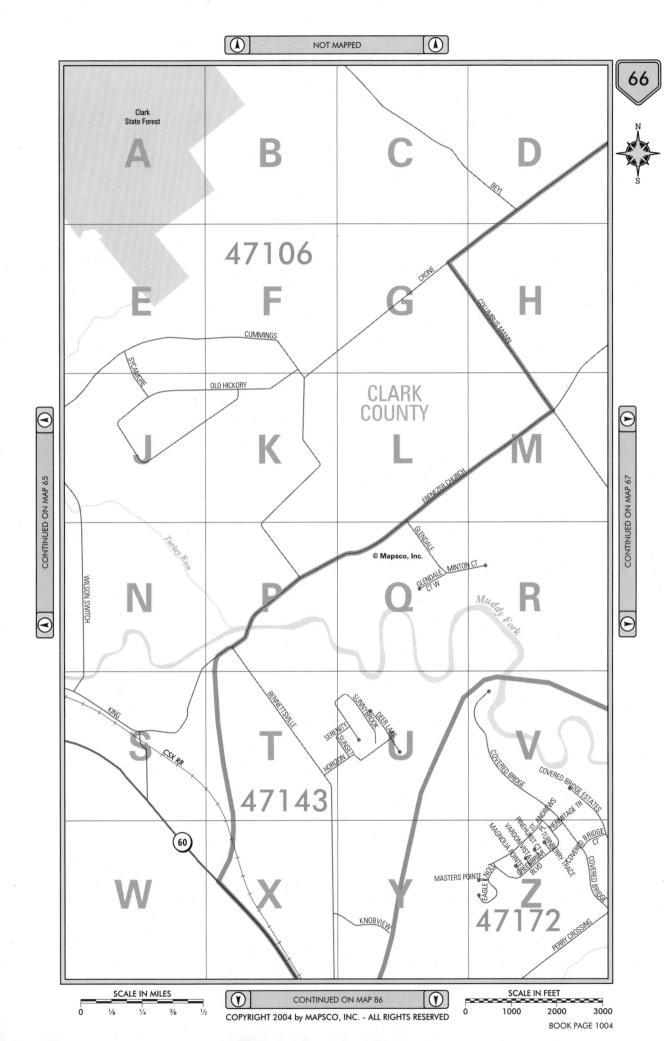

66

Clark
State Forest

A B C D

47106

E F G H

BEYL

CRONE

COLUMBUS-MANN

CUMMINGS

SYCAMORE

OLD HICKORY

CLARK
COUNTY

J K L M

EBENEZER CHURCH

Turkey Run

GLENDALE

© Mapsco, Inc.

GLENDALE
CT W

MINTON CT

WILSON SWITCH

N P Q R

Muddy Fork

CONTINUED ON MAP 65

CONTINUED ON MAP 67

KING

BENNETTSVILLE

SUNNY BROOK

DEER LAKE

SERENITY

SUNSET

HORIZON

COVERED BRIDGE

COVERED BRIDGE ESTATES

S T U V

CSX RR

47143

60

ST ANDREWS

HERMITAGE TR

PINEHURST CT

TURNBERRY TRACE

COVERED BRIDGE
CT

VARDON VISTA

GREENBRIAR

MAGNOLIA POINTE

BLVD

COVERED BRIDGE

MASTERS POINTE

EAGLE KNOLL

W X Y Z

47172

KNOBVIEW

PERRY CROSSING

SCALE IN MILES
0   1/8   1/4   3/8   1/2

SCALE IN FEET
0   1000   2000   3000

BOOK PAGE 1004

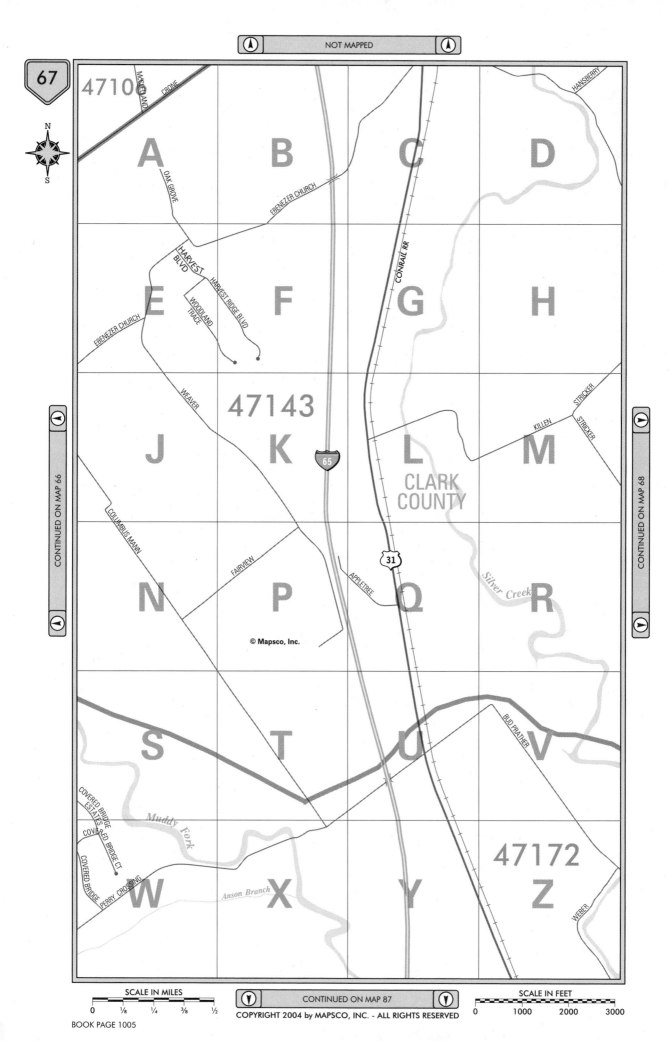

67

4710

N
S

NOT MAPPED

CONTINUED ON MAP 66

CONTINUED ON MAP 68

CONTINUED ON MAP 87

A B C D

E F G H

J K L M

N P Q R

S T U V

W X Y Z

47143

CLARK COUNTY

47172

MCCLELLAND
CRONE
OAK GROVE
EBENEZER CHURCH
HANSBERRY
CONRAIL RR
HARVEST BLVD
HARVEST RIDGE BLVD
WOODLAND TRACE
EBENEZER CHURCH
WEAVER
KILLEN
STRICKER
STRICKER
COLUMBUS MANN
FAIRVIEW
APPLETREE
Silver Creek
BUD PRATHER
COVERED BRIDGE ESTATES
COVERED BRIDGE CT
COVERED BRIDGE
PERRY CROSSING
Muddy Fork
Anson Branch
WEBER

65

31

SCALE IN MILES
0 1/8 1/4 3/8 1/2

SCALE IN FEET
0 1000 2000 3000

BOOK PAGE 1005

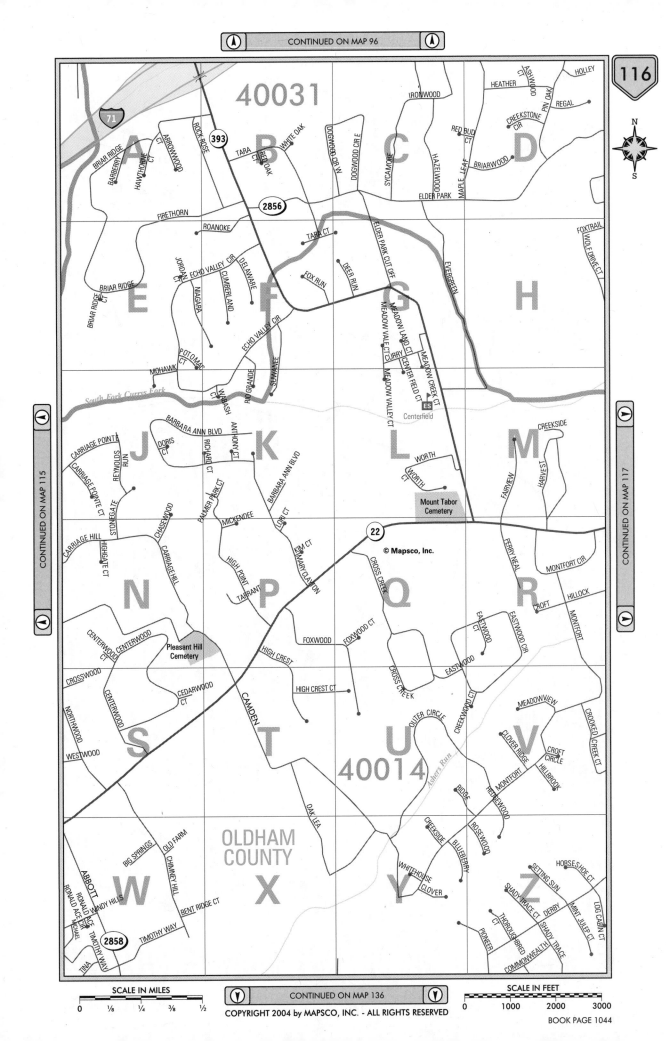

116

40031

40014

OLDHAM COUNTY

© Mapsco, Inc.

Mount Tabor Cemetery

Pleasant Hill Cemetery

Centerfield

CONTINUED ON MAP 115

CONTINUED ON MAP 117

SCALE IN MILES

0   1/8   1/4   3/8   1/2

CONTINUED ON MAP 136

SCALE IN FEET

0   1000   2000   3000

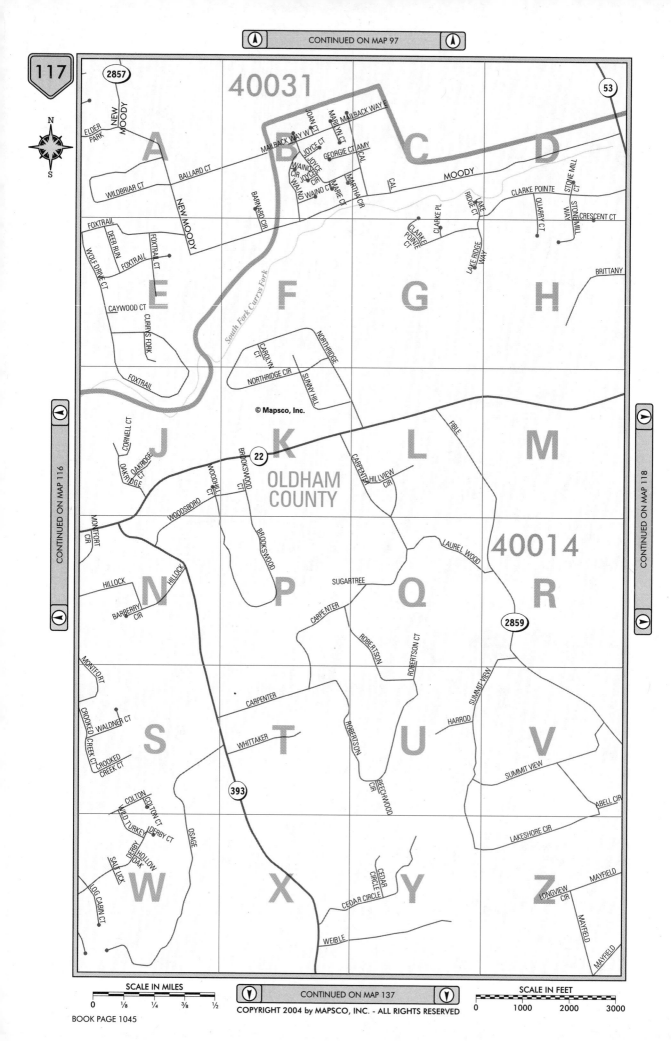

117

2857

40031

53

N
S

A

NEW MOODY

ELDER PARK

WILDBRIAR CT

BALLARD CT

NEW MOODY

B

JOAN CT

MAILBACK WAY W

MARILYN CT

MAILBACK WAY E

JOYCE CT

JOYCE CIR

GEORGIE CT AMY

WAINO CIR

WAINO JOYCE

WAINO C

BARNARD CIR

MARTHA CIR

MARIE CT

CAL

CAL

C

MOODY

D

STONE MILL CT

CLARKE POINTE

QUARRY CT

STONE MILL WAY

CRESCENT CT

CLARKE PL

LAKE RIDGE CT

FOXTRAIL

DEER RUN

FOXTRAIL

WOLF DRIVE CT

FOXTRAIL CT

CAYWOOD CT

CURRY'S FORK

FOXTRAIL

E

F

CLARKE POINTE CT

LAKE RIDGE WAY

G

H

BRITTANY

South Fork Currys Fork

CAROLYN CT

NORTHRIDGE CIR

NORTHRIDGE

SUNNY HILL

© Mapsco, Inc.

FIBLE

CORNELL CT

OAKRIDGE CT

OAKRIDGE

J

MOODYHILL

WOODSBORO

BROOKSWOOD CT

22

K

OLDHAM COUNTY

CARPENTER

HILLVIEW CIR

L

M

40014

MONTFORT CIR

HILLOCK

HILLOCK

BARBERRY CIR

N

BROOKSWOOD

P

SUGARTREE

CARPENTER

Q

ROBERTSON

LAUREL WOOD

ROBERTSON CT

R

2859

MONTFORT

CROOKED CREEK CT

WALDNER CT

CROOKED CREEK CT

S

CARPENTER

WHITTAKER

T

ROBERTSON

U

ROBERTSON CIR

BEECHWOOD

HARROD

SUMMIT VIEW

SUMMIT VIEW

V

SUMMIT VIEW

ABELL CIR

393

COLTON

COLTON CT

DERBY CT

WILD TURKEY

DERBY HOLLOW

OAK

SALT LICK

OSAGE

LOG CABIN CT

W

X

CEDAR CIRCLE

CEDAR CIRCLE

Y

WEIBLE

LAKESHORE CIR

Z

LONGVIEW CIR

MAYFIELD

MAYFIELD

MAYFIELD

CONTINUED ON MAP 116

CONTINUED ON MAP 118

SCALE IN MILES

0   1/8   1/4   3/8   1/2

SCALE IN FEET

0   1000   2000   3000

BOOK PAGE 1045

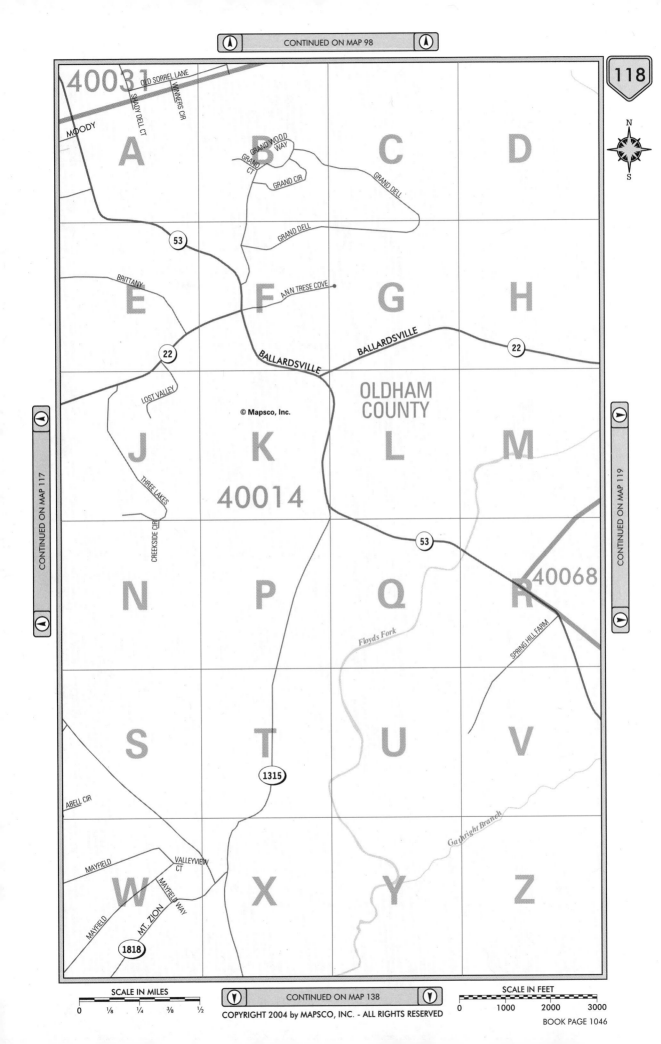

CONTINUED ON MAP 98

118

40031

OLD SORREL LANE

WINNERS CIR

SHADY DELL CT

MOODY

A

B

GRAND WOOD WAY

GRAND CT

GRAND CIR

C

GRAND DELL

D

53

BRITTANY

GRAND DELL

E

F

ANN TRESE COVE

G

H

BALLARDSVILLE

BALLARDSVILLE

22

22

LOST VALLEY

© Mapsco, Inc.

OLDHAM
COUNTY

J

K

L

M

THREE LAKES

40014

CREEKSIDE CIR

53

N

P

Q

R

40068

Floyds Fork

SPRING HILL FARM

ABELL CIR

S

T

U

V

1315

Gathright Branch

MAYFIELD

VALLEYVIEW CT

MAYFIELD WAY

W

X

Y

Z

MAYFIELD

MT. ZION

1818

N

S

CONTINUED ON MAP 117

CONTINUED ON MAP 119

SCALE IN MILES

0   ⅛   ¼   ⅜   ½

CONTINUED ON MAP 138

SCALE IN FEET

0   1000   2000   3000

BOOK PAGE 1046

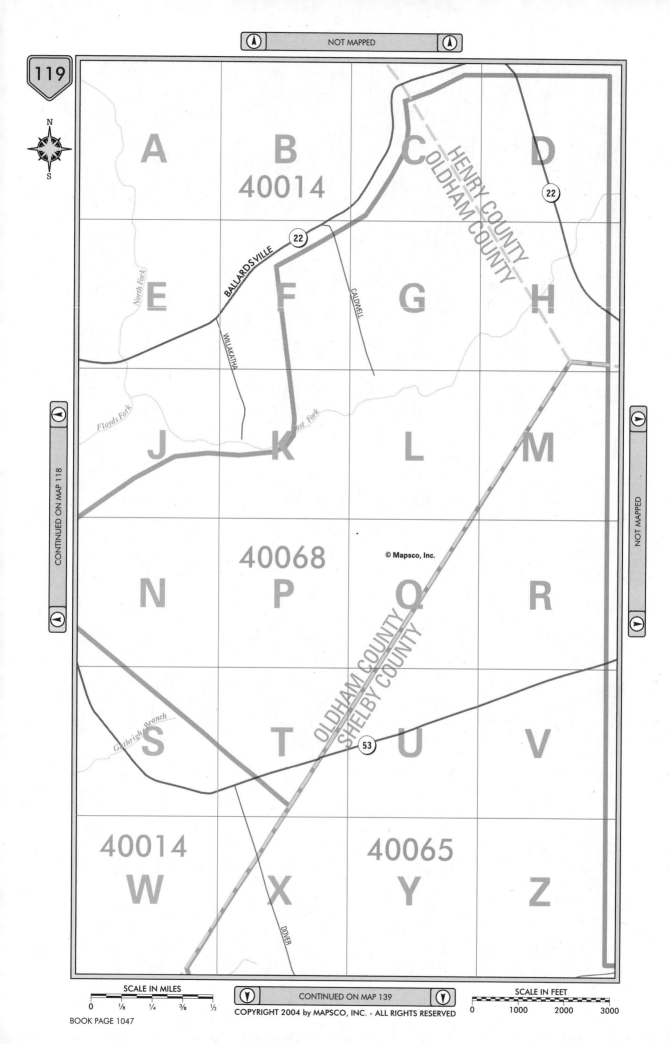

NOT MAPPED

CONTINUED ON MAP 118

NOT MAPPED

CONTINUED ON MAP 139

N
S

A

B
40014

C

HENRY COUNTY
COLDHAM COUNTY

D

22

BALLARDSVILLE

22

E

F

CALDWELL

G

H

North Fork

WILLAKATHA

Floyds Fork

J

East Fork

K

L

M

40068

© Mapsco, Inc.

N

P

OLDHAM COUNTY
SHELBY COUNTY

Q

R

Guthright Branch

S

T

53

U

V

40014

W

X

DOVER

40065

Y

Z

SCALE IN MILES

0   1/8   1/4   3/8   1/2

SCALE IN FEET

0   1000   2000   3000

BOOK PAGE 1047

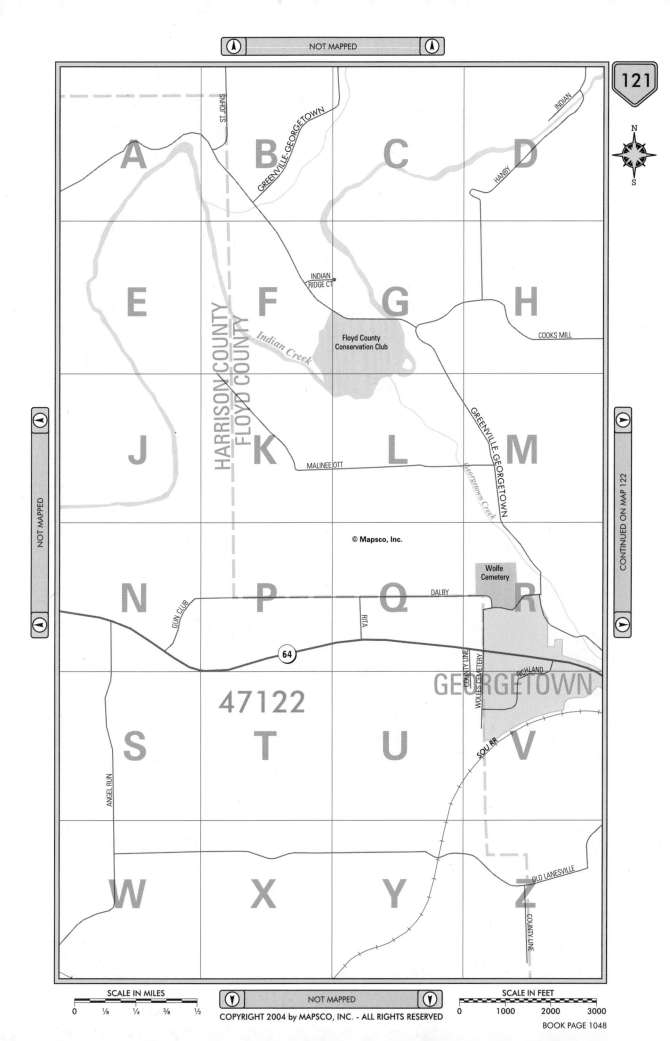

121

N
W — E
S

A

B

C

INDIAN

D

HANBY

GREENVILLE-GEORGETOWN

ST. JOHNS

E

F

INDIAN
RIDGE CT

Indian Creek

G

Floyd County
Conservation Club

H

COOKS MILL

HARRISON COUNTY
FLOYD COUNTY

J

K

MALINEE OTT

L

GREENVILLE-GEORGETOWN

Georgetown Creek

M

N

GUN CLUB

P

Q

RITA

DALBY

Wolfe
Cemetery

R

64

COUNTY LINE

WOLFE CEMETERY

RICHLAND

GEORGETOWN

47122

S

ANGEL RUN

T

U

SOU RR

V

W

X

Y

OLD LANESVILLE

Z

COUNTY LINE

NOT MAPPED

SCALE IN MILES
0   1/8   1/4   3/8   1/2

SCALE IN FEET
0   1000   2000   3000

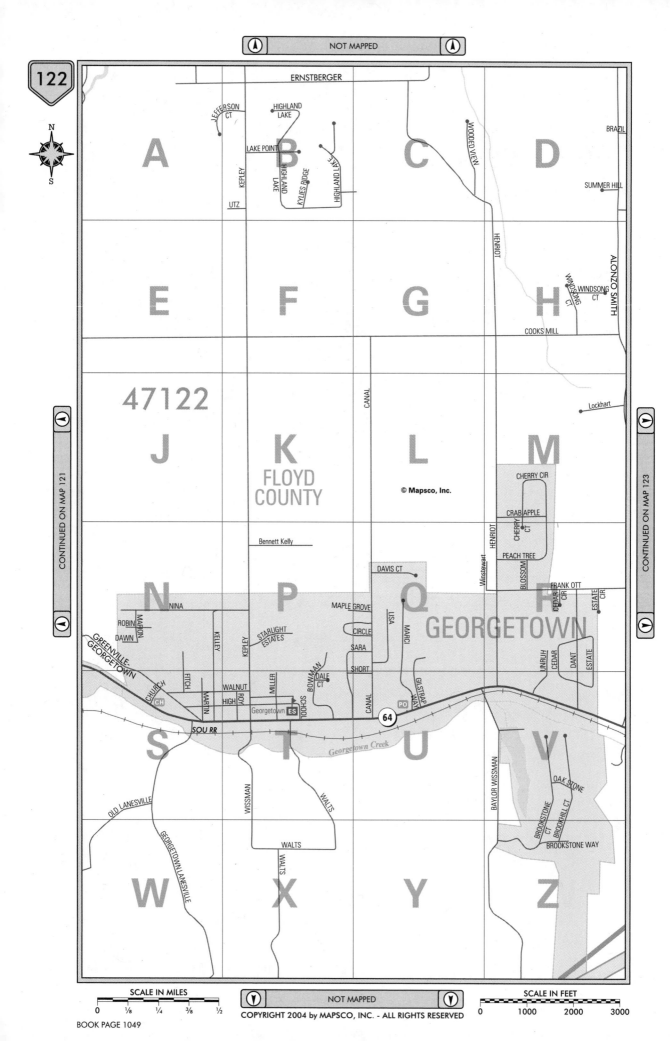

122

N
W E
S

ERNSTBERGER

JEFFERSON CT

HIGHLAND LAKE

A   B   C   D

LAKE POINT

KEPLEY

HIGHLAND LAKE

KYLES RIDGE

UTZ

HIGHLAND LAKE

BRAZIL

WOODED VIEW

SUMMER HILL

HENRIOT

ALONZO SMITH

E   F   G   H

WINDSONG CT
WINDSONG CT

COOKS MILL

47122

CANAL

LOCKHART

J   K   L   M

FLOYD COUNTY

CHERRY CIR

CRAB APPLE

CHERRY CT

BENNETT KELLY

PEACH TREE

HENRIOT

Winstewart

BLOSSOM CT

DAVIS CT

FRANK OTT

N   P   Q   R

NINA

MARION

ROBIN

DAWN

KELLEY

KEPLEY

STARLIGHT ESTATES

MAPLE GROVE

CIRCLE

LISA

MARCI

GEORGETOWN

CEDAR CIR

ESTATE CIR

SARA

SHORT

BOWMAN

DALE CT

UNRUH

CEDAR

DANT

ESTATE

GREENVILLE GEORGETOWN

CHURCH

CH

FITCH

MARTIN

WALNUT

HIGH

ROY

MILLER

SCHOSS

Georgetown ES

CANAL

GILSTRAP WAY

PO

64

SOU RR

S   T   U   V

Georgetown Creek

BAYLOR WISSMAN

OAK STONE

WISSMAN

WALTS

BROOKSTONE CT

BROOKHILL CT

OLD LANESVILLE

GEORGETOWN LANESVILLE

WALTS

WALTS

BROOKSTONE WAY

W   X   Y   Z

CONTINUED ON MAP 121

CONTINUED ON MAP 123

SCALE IN MILES
0   1/8   1/4   3/8   1/2

SCALE IN FEET
0   1000   2000   3000

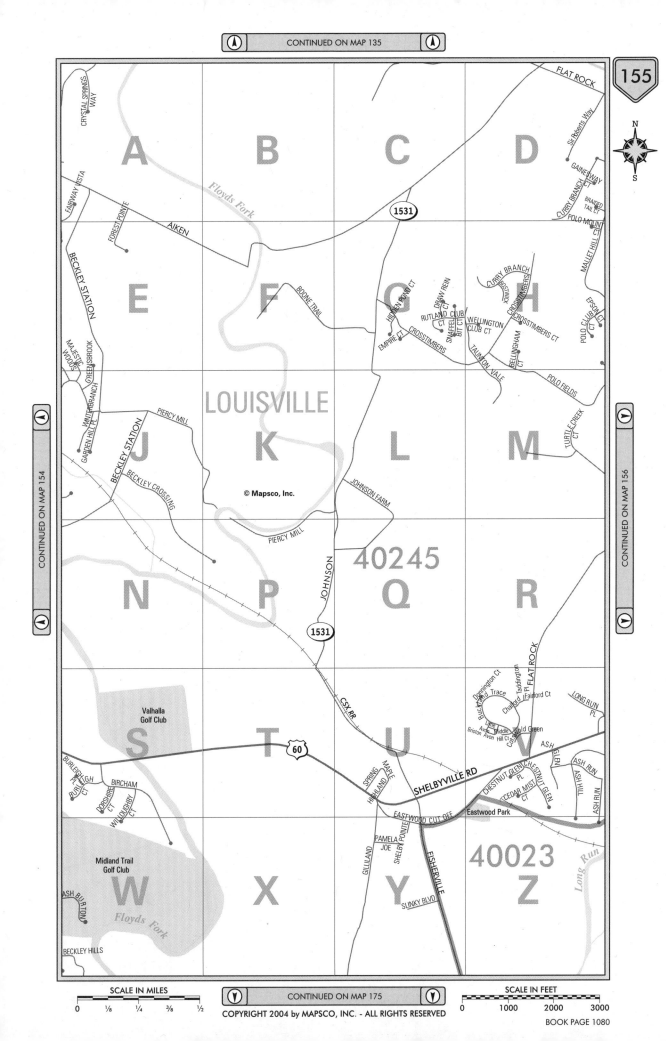

155

N
S

A
B
C
D

CRYSTAL SPRINGS WAY

FLAT ROCK

Sir Roberts Way

GAINESWAY CT

FAIRWAY VISTA

Floyds Fork

1531

CURRY BRANCH

BRAIDED TAIL CT

FOREST POINTE

AIKEN

POLO MOUNT CT

MALLET HILL

BECKLEY STATION

E
F
G
H

BOONE TRAIL

CURRY BRANCH

BESTWICK

EPSON CT

HIDDEN POND CT

DRAW REIN

CROSSTIMBERS

POLO CLUB CT

MAJESTIC WOODS

RUTLAND CLUB CT

SNAFFEL CT

BIT CT

CROSSTIMBERS CT

GREENSBROOK

EMPIRE CT

CROSSTIMBERS

WELLINGTON CLUB CT

BELLINGHAM CT

WINTERBRANCH

TAUNTON VALE

POLO FIELDS

GARDEN HILL PL

PIERCY MILL

LOUISVILLE

J
K
L
M

BECKLEY STATION

TURTLE CREEK CT

BECKLEY CROSSING

JOHNSON FARM

© Mapsco, Inc.

PIERCY MILL

40245

N
P
Q
R

JOHNSON

CONTINUED ON MAP 154

CONTINUED ON MAP 156

1531

CSX RR

FLAT ROCK

Dinnington Ct

Taddington

Charford Pl

LONG RUN PL

Buckland Trace

Fairford Ct

Valhalla Golf Club

Little Avon

Middle Avon

Cotswold Green

S
T
U
V

Briston Avon

Hill Ct

60

ASH GLEN

BURLEIGH PL CT

SPRING

MAPLE

CHESTNUT GLEN PL

ASH RUN

BIRCHAM

HIGHLAND

SHELBYVILLE RD

CHESTNUT GLEN

ASH HILL

DORSHIRE CT

CEDAR MIST CT

ASH RUN

WILLOUGHBY CT

EASTWOOD CUT OFF

Eastwood Park

Midland Trail Golf Club

PAMELA

40023

ASH BURTON

JOE

GILLILAND

SHELBY POINTE

FISHERVILLE

Long Run

W
X
Y
Z

Floyds Fork

SLINKY BLVD

BECKLEY HILLS

SCALE IN MILES

0   1/8   1/4   3/8   1/2

SCALE IN FEET

0   1000   2000   3000

BOOK PAGE 1080

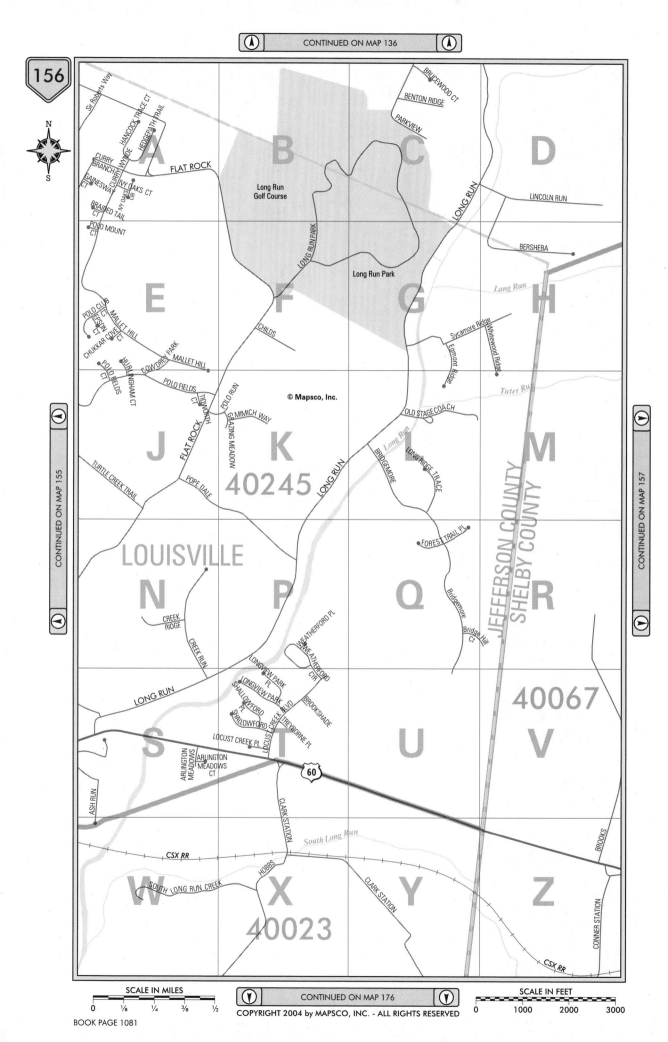

156

N
S

CONTINUED ON MAP 155

CONTINUED ON MAP 157

Sir Roberts Way
HANCOCK TRACE CT
HEDGEPATH TRAIL
CURRY WYNDE
CURRY BRANCH
GAINESWAY CT
CURRY WYNDE CT
IVY OAKS CT
BRAIDED TAIL CT
POLO MOUNT CT

A
FLAT ROCK

BRICEWOOD CT
BENTON RIDGE
PARKVIEW

B

C

D
LINCOLN RUN

LONG RUN
BERSHEBA

Long Run
Golf Course

LONG RUN PARK

Long Run Park

Lang Run

E
F
G
H

POLO CLUB
JEFFERSON CT
MALLET HILL
CHUKKAR COVE CT
POLO FIELDS
HURLINGHAM CT
COWDREY PARK
MALLET HILL

CHILDS

Sycamore Ridge
Whitewood Ridge
Egmont Ridge

Tater Run

POLO FIELDS CT
TIDNORTH
POLO RUN
GRAZING MEADOW
MIMICH WAY

© Mapsco, Inc.

OLD STAGE COACH

Long Run

BRIDGEMORE
LONG RIDGE TRACE

JEFFERSON COUNTY
SHELBY COUNTY

J
FLAT ROCK

K

40245

LONG RUN

L

M

TURTLE CREEK TRAIL
POPE DALE

FOREST TRAIL PL

Bridgemore

LOUISVILLE

N
P
Q
R

40067

CREEK RIDGE
CREEK RUN

WEATHERFORD PL
WEATHERFORD CTR
LONGVIEW PARK PL
LONGVIEW PARK BLVD
SHALLOWFORD PL
SHALLOWFORD PL
BROOKSHADE
LOCUST CREEK BLVD
TREYBORNE PL
LOCUST CREEK PL

Bridge Hill Ct

LONG RUN

V

ASH RUN
ARLINGTON MEADOWS
ARLINGTON MEADOWS CT

S
T

60

U

CLARK STATION

CSX RR

HOBBS
South Long Run

CLARK STATION

BROOKS

W
SOUTH LONG RUN CREEK
X
40023
Y
Z
CONNER STATION
CSX RR

SCALE IN MILES
0   1/8   1/4   3/8   1/2

CONTINUED ON MAP 176

SCALE IN FEET
0   1000   2000   3000

BOOK PAGE 1081   COPYRIGHT 2004 by MAPSCO, INC. - ALL RIGHTS RESERVED

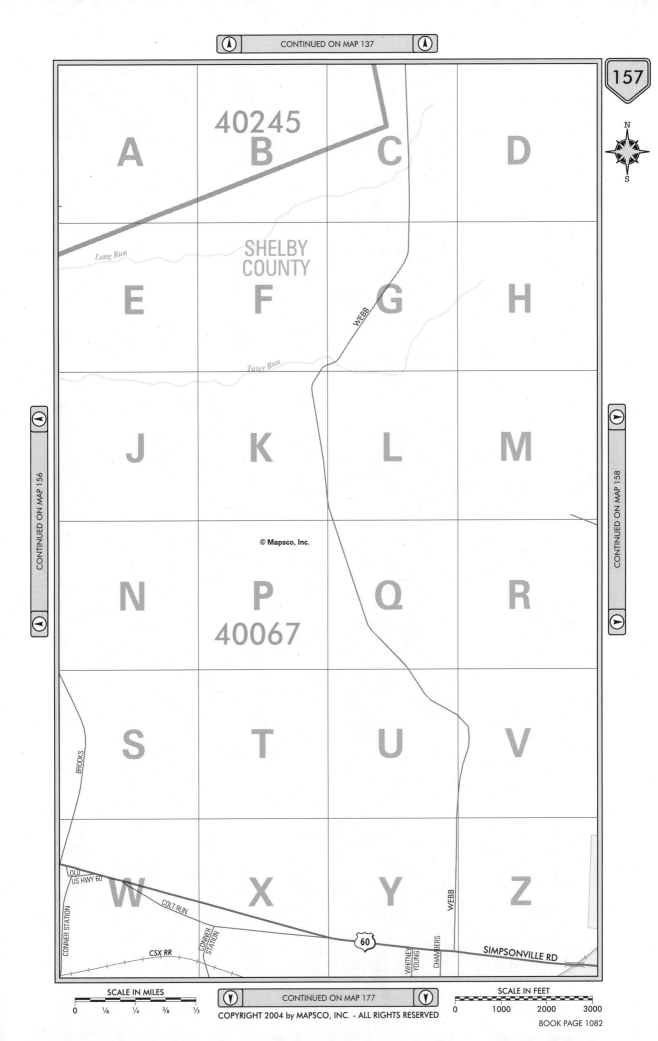

CONTINUED ON MAP 137

157

N
S

40245

A　　B　　C　　D

SHELBY
COUNTY

Lang Run

E　　F　　G　　H

WEBB

Tater Run

CONTINUED ON MAP 156

J　　K　　L　　M

CONTINUED ON MAP 158

© Mapsco, Inc.

N　　P　　Q　　R

40067

BROOKS

S　　T　　U　　V

OLD
US HWY 60

W　　X　　Y　　Z

COLT RUN

WEBB

CONNER STATION

CONNER STATION

CSX RR

60

WHITNEY YOUNG

CHAMBERS

SIMPSONVILLE RD

SCALE IN MILES

0　　⅛　　¼　　⅜　　½

CONTINUED ON MAP 177

SCALE IN FEET

0　　1000　　2000　　3000

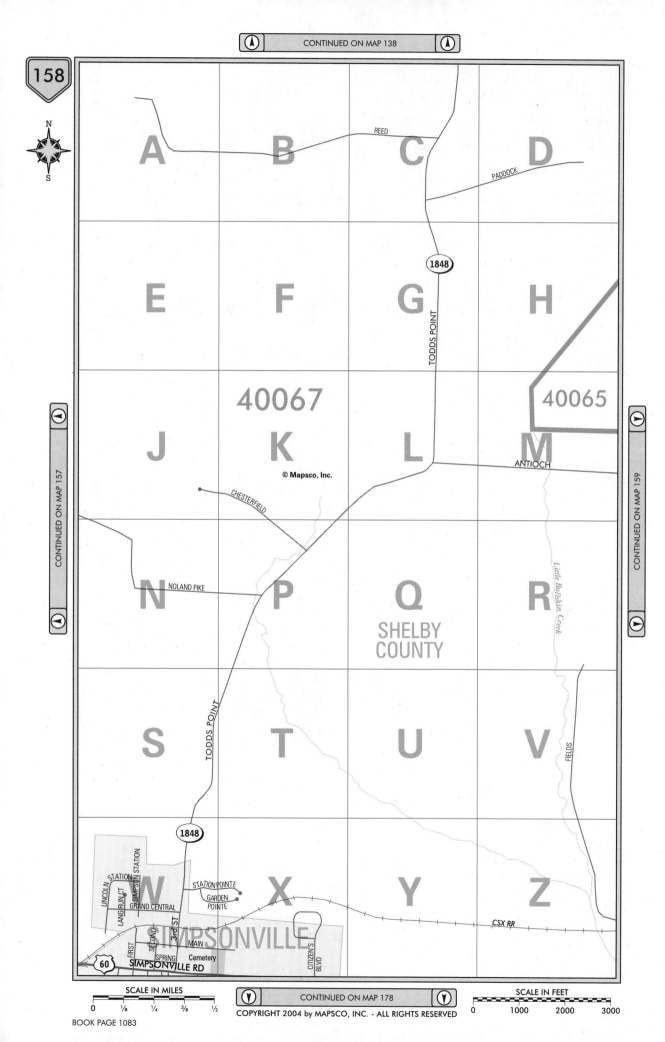

158

N
W E
S

A B C D

REED

PADDOCK

1848

E F G H

TODDS POINT

CONTINUED ON MAP 157

CONTINUED ON MAP 159

40067

40065

J K L M

© Mapsco, Inc.

ANTIOCH

CHESTERFIELD

N P Q R

NOLAND PIKE

SHELBY
COUNTY

Little Bullskin Creek

S T U V

TODDS POINT

FIELDS

1848

LINCOLN STATION
SIMPSON STATION
STATION POINTE
LANGRUN CT
GRAND CENTRAL
GARDEN POINTE

W X Y Z

3rd ST

SIMPSONVILLE

CSX RR

FIRST
SECOND
SPRING
MAIN
Cemetery
CITIZEN'S BLVD

60
SIMPSONVILLE RD

SCALE IN MILES

0 ⅛ ¼ ⅜ ½

CONTINUED ON MAP 178

SCALE IN FEET

0 1000 2000 3000

BOOK PAGE 1083

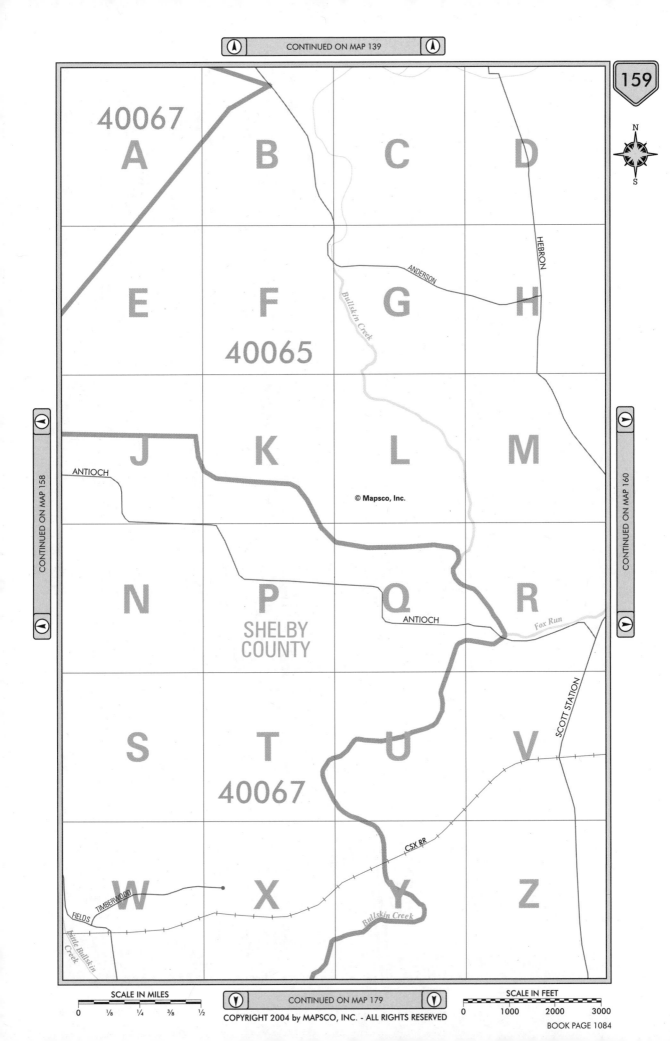

159

N
S

40067

A   B   C   D

HEBRON

ANDERSON

E   F   G   H

Bullskin Creek

40065

CONTINUED ON MAP 158
CONTINUED ON MAP 160

J   K   L   M

ANTIOCH

© Mapsco, Inc.

N   P   Q   R

SHELBY
COUNTY

ANTIOCH   Fox Run

S   T   U   V

SCOTT STATION

40067

CSX RR

W   X   Y   Z

TIMBERWOOD

FIELDS

Bullskin Creek

Little Bullskin
Creek

SCALE IN MILES
0   ⅛   ¼   ⅜   ½

SCALE IN FEET
0   1000   2000   3000

BOOK PAGE 1084

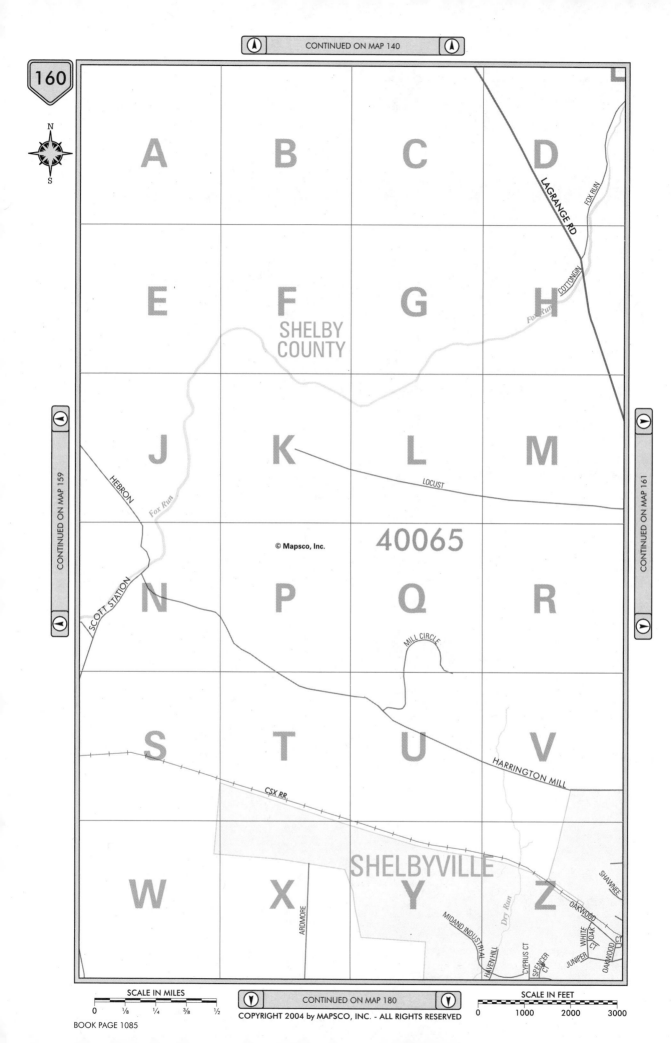

CONTINUED ON MAP 140

160

N
S

CONTINUED ON MAP 159

CONTINUED ON MAP 161

A   B   C   D

LAGRANGE RD
FOX RUN

E   F   G   H
SHELBY
COUNTY
COTTONGIN
Fox Run

J   K   L   M
HEBRON
Fox Run
LOCUST

© Mapsco, Inc.   40065

N   P   Q   R
SCOTT STATION
MILL CIRCLE

S   T   U   V
HARRINGTON MILL

CSX RR.

SHELBYVILLE

W   X   Y   Z
ARDMORE
SHAWNEE
OAKWOOD
MIDAND INDUSTRIAL
Dry Run
WHITE
OAK
OAKWOOD CT
HAVEN HILL
CYPRUS CT
SPENCER CT
JUNIPER

SCALE IN MILES
0   1/8   1/4   3/8   1/2

CONTINUED ON MAP 180

SCALE IN FEET
0   1000   2000   3000

BOOK PAGE 1085

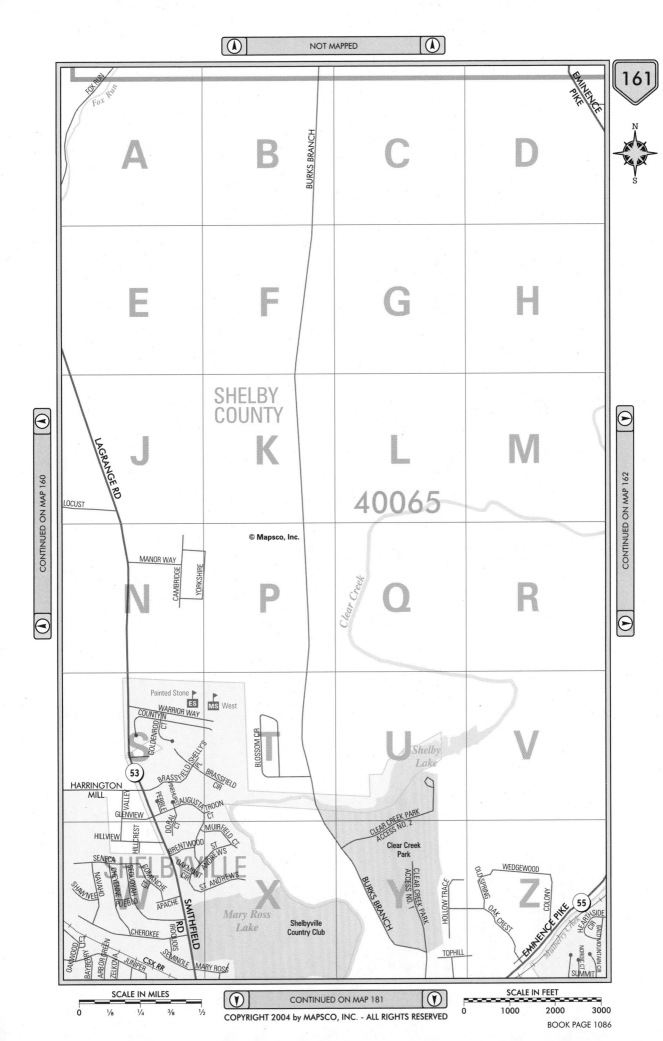

161

N
S

A B C D

FOX RUN
Fox Run

BURKS BRANCH

EMINENCE PIKE

E F G H

CONTINUED ON MAP 160

CONTINUED ON MAP 162

SHELBY COUNTY

J K L M

LAGRANGE RD

LOCUST

40065

© Mapsco, Inc.

MANOR WAY

CAMBRIDGE YORKSHIRE

N P Q R

Clear Creek

Painted Stone ES MS West

WARRIOR WAY
COUNTY IN

GOLDENROD CT

BLOSSOM CIR

Shelby Lake

S T U V

53

HARRINGTON MILL

BRASSFIELD
SHELLY'S PL
BRASSFIELD CIR

PERBLE
VALLEY
PINEHURST
AUGUSTA
TROON CT
DORAL CT
MUIRFIELD CT

GLENVIEW

HILLVIEW HILLCREST

BRENTWOOD

CLEAR CREEK PARK
ACCESS NO. 2

Clear Creek Park

ST ANDREWS

SENECA

NAVAHO

CHEYENNE
SEQUOYAH

COMANCHE

OAKMONT CIR
ST ANDREWS

SHELBYVILLE

W X Y Z

CLEAR CREEK PARK ACCESS NO. 1

WEDGEWOOD

OLD SPRING COLONY

55

SHAWNEE
PUEBLO
APACHE

SMITHFIELD RD

BURKS BRANCH

HOLLOW TRACE

OAK CREST

EMINENCE PIKE

Mulberry Creek

CHEROKEE

IROQUOIS

Mary Ross Lake

Shelbyville Country Club

HEARTHSIDE CIR
BALD MOUNTAIN CIR

OAKWOOD CT
BAYBERRY
ARBOR GREEN
ZELKOVA
JUNIPER

CSX RR
SEMINOLE
MARY ROSS

TOPHILL

NORDIC CT
SUMMIT

SCALE IN MILES
0 1/8 1/4 3/8 1/2

CONTINUED ON MAP 181

SCALE IN FEET
0 1000 2000 3000

BOOK PAGE 1086

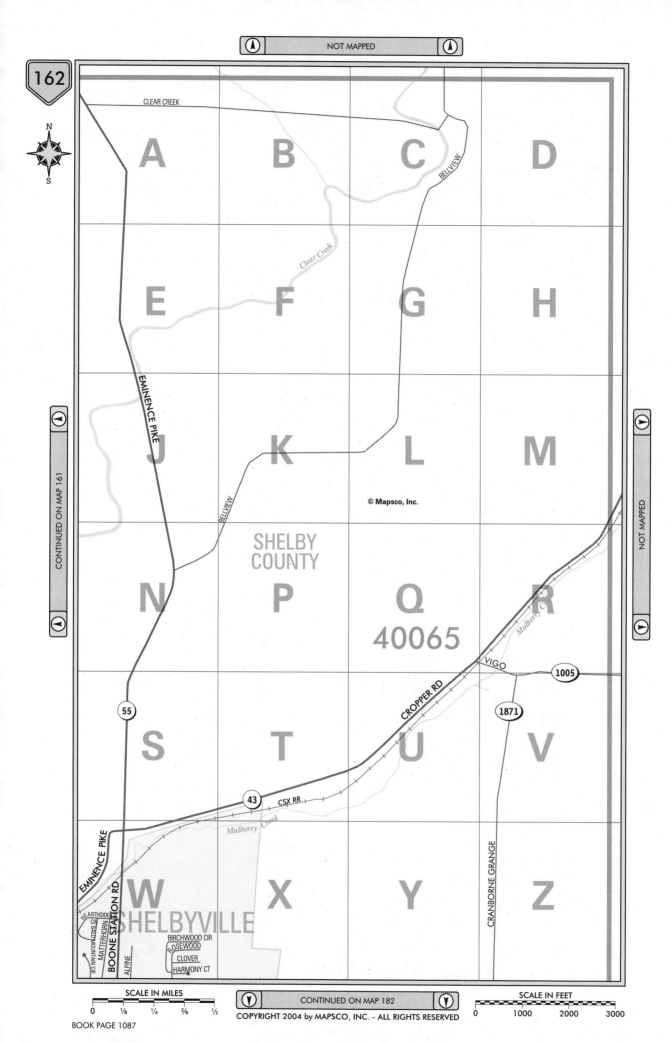

NOT MAPPED

N

S

CLEAR CREEK

A   B   C   D

Clear Creek

BELLVIEW

E   F   G   H

CONTINUED ON MAP 161

EMINENCE PIKE

J   K   L   M

NOT MAPPED

BELLVIEW

© Mapsco, Inc.

SHELBY
COUNTY

N   P   Q   R

40065

Mulberry Creek

VIGO   1005

CROPPER RD

1871

55

S   T   U   V

43   CSX RR

Mulberry Creek

CRANBORNE GRANGE

EMINENCE PIKE

W   X   Y   Z

BOONE STATION RD

HEARTHSIDE CIR
MATTERHORN CIR
BALTUSROL
UNION
ALPINE

SHELBYVILLE

BIRCHWOOD CIR
ROSEWOOD
CLOVER
HARMONY CT

SCALE IN MILES

0   1/8   1/4   3/8   1/2

CONTINUED ON MAP 182

SCALE IN FEET

0   1000   2000   3000

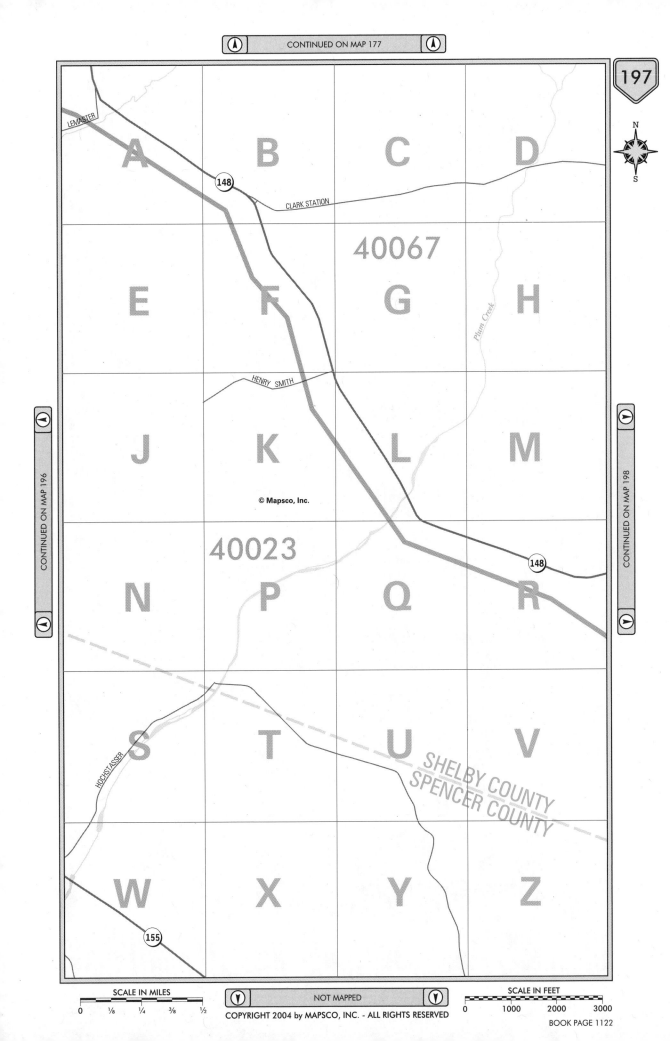

197

N
S

LEMASTER

A

148

B

C

D

CLARK STATION

40067

E

F

G

Plum Creek

H

HENRY SMITH

J

K

L

M

© Mapsco, Inc.

40023

N

P

Q

148

R

HOCHSTASSER

S

T

U

SHELBY COUNTY
SPENCER COUNTY

V

W

155

X

Y

Z

SCALE IN MILES

0   ⅛   ¼   ⅜   ½

NOT MAPPED

SCALE IN FEET

0   1000   2000   3000

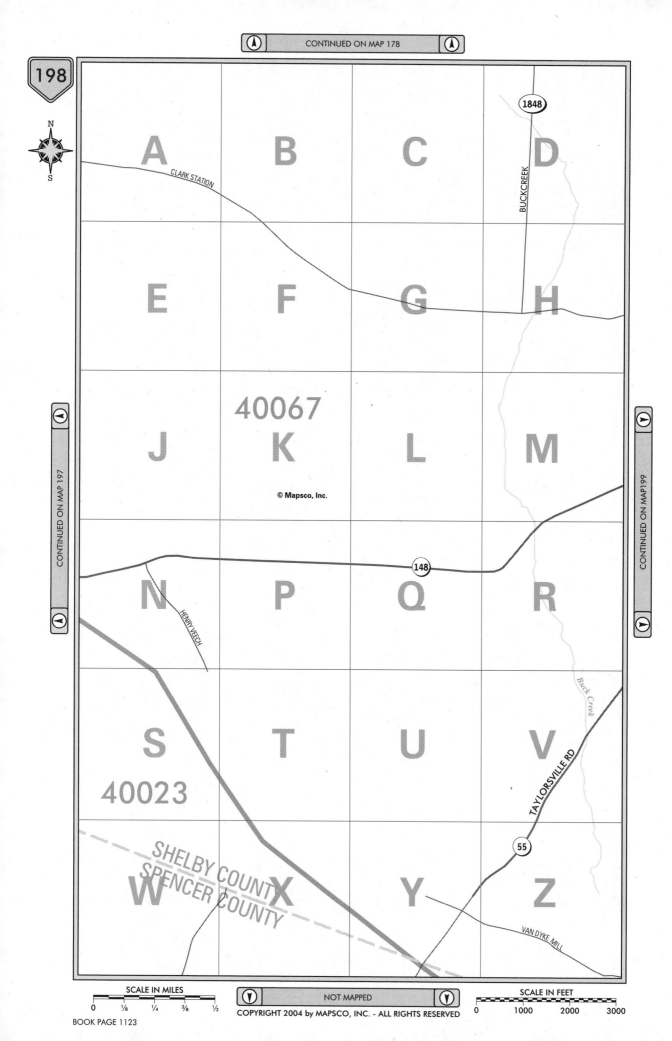

CONTINUED ON MAP 178

198

N
S

A B C D

1848

CLARK STATION

BUCKCREEK

E F G H

40067

CONTINUED ON MAP 197

CONTINUED ON MAP199

J K L M

© Mapsco, Inc.

148

N P Q R

HENRY VEECH

Buck Creek

S T U V

TAYLORSVILLE RD

40023

55

SHELBY COUNTY
SPENCER COUNTY

W X Y Z

VAN DYKE MILL

SCALE IN MILES
0   1/8   1/4   3/8   1/2

NOT MAPPED

SCALE IN FEET
0   1000   2000   3000

BOOK PAGE 1123

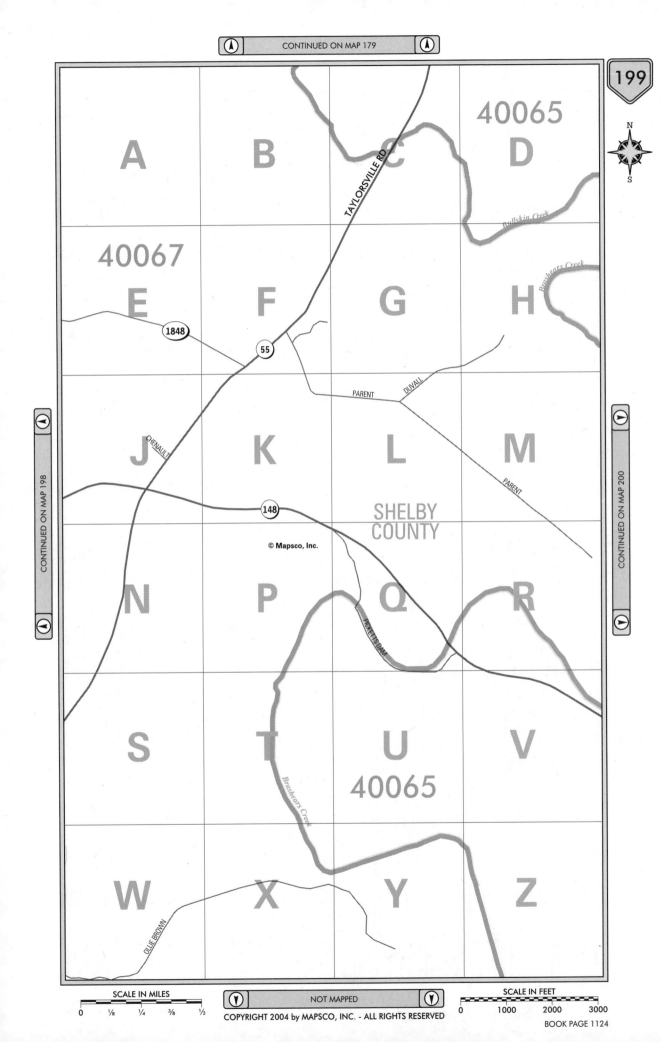

CONTINUED ON MAP 179

199

40065

A B C D

N

40067

E F G H

TAYLORSVILLE RD

Bullskin Creek

Brashears Creek

1848

55

PARENT DUVALL

J K L M

CHENAULT

PARENT

148

SHELBY
COUNTY

© Mapsco, Inc.

N P Q R

PICKETTS DAM

S T U V

Brashears Creek

40065

W X Y Z

OLLIE BROWN

CONTINUED ON MAP 198

CONTINUED ON MAP 200

SCALE IN MILES

0   ⅛   ¼   ⅜   ½

NOT MAPPED

SCALE IN FEET

0   1000   2000   3000

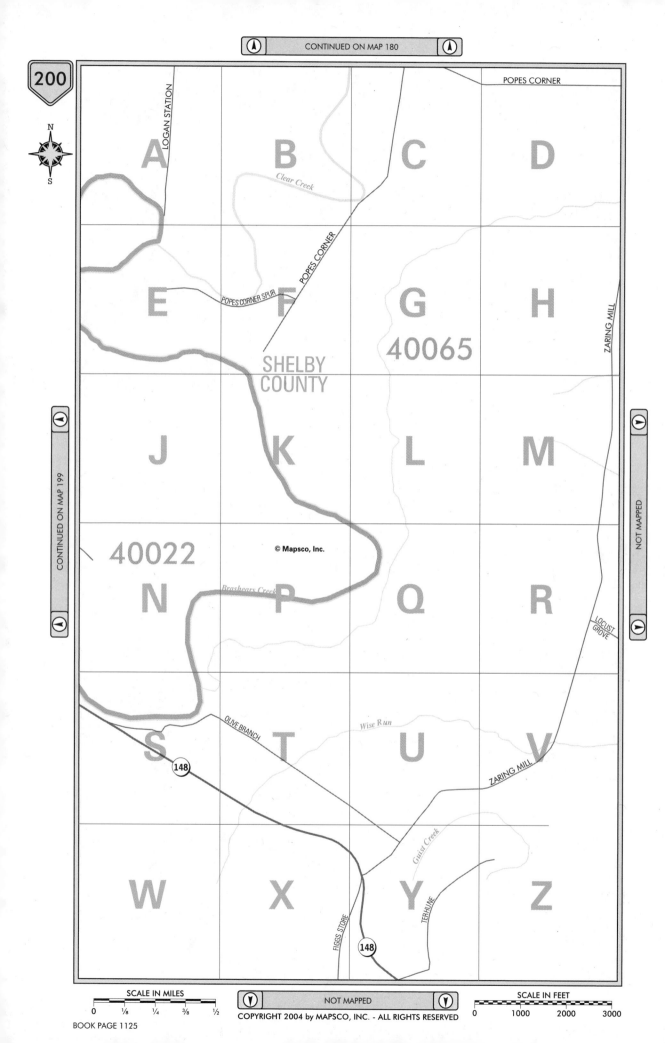

CONTINUED ON MAP 180

200

POPES CORNER

LOGAN STATION

A   B   C   D

Clear Creek

POPES CORNER

POPES CORNER SPUR

E   F   G   H

ZARING MILL

40065

SHELBY
COUNTY

CONTINUED ON MAP 199

J   K   L   M

NOT MAPPED

40022

© Mapsco, Inc.

N   P   Q   R

Brashears Creek

LOCUST
GROVE

OLIVE BRANCH   Wise Run

S   T   U   V

ZARING MILL

148

Guist Creek

W   X   Y   Z

TERHUNE

FIGGS STORE

148

SCALE IN MILES

0   1/8   1/4   3/8   1/2

NOT MAPPED

SCALE IN FEET

0   1000   2000   3000

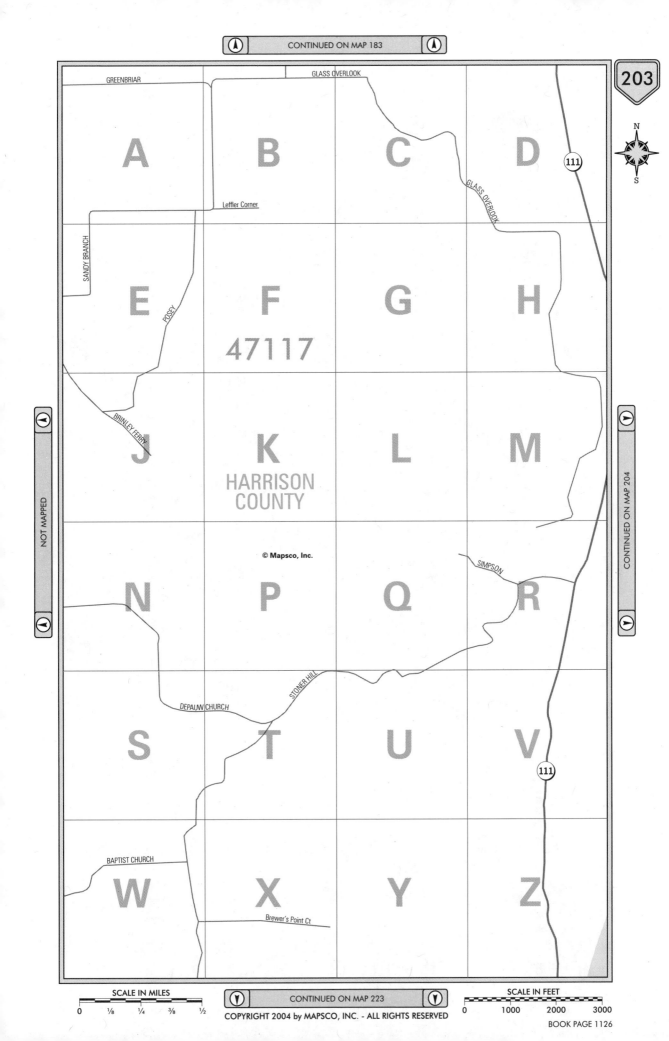

203

N
S

GREENBRIAR

GLASS OVERLOOK

A

B

C

D

111

Leffler Corner

SANDY BRANCH

E

F

G

H

POSEY

GLASS OVERLOOK

47117

BRINLEY FERRY

J

K

L

M

HARRISON
COUNTY

SIMPSON

© Mapsco, Inc.

N

P

Q

R

STONER HILL

DEPAUW CHURCH

S

T

U

V

111

BAPTIST CHURCH

W

X

Y

Z

Brewer's Point Ct

NOT MAPPED

CONTINUED ON MAP 204

SCALE IN MILES

0   ⅛   ¼   ⅜   ½

SCALE IN FEET

0   1000   2000   3000

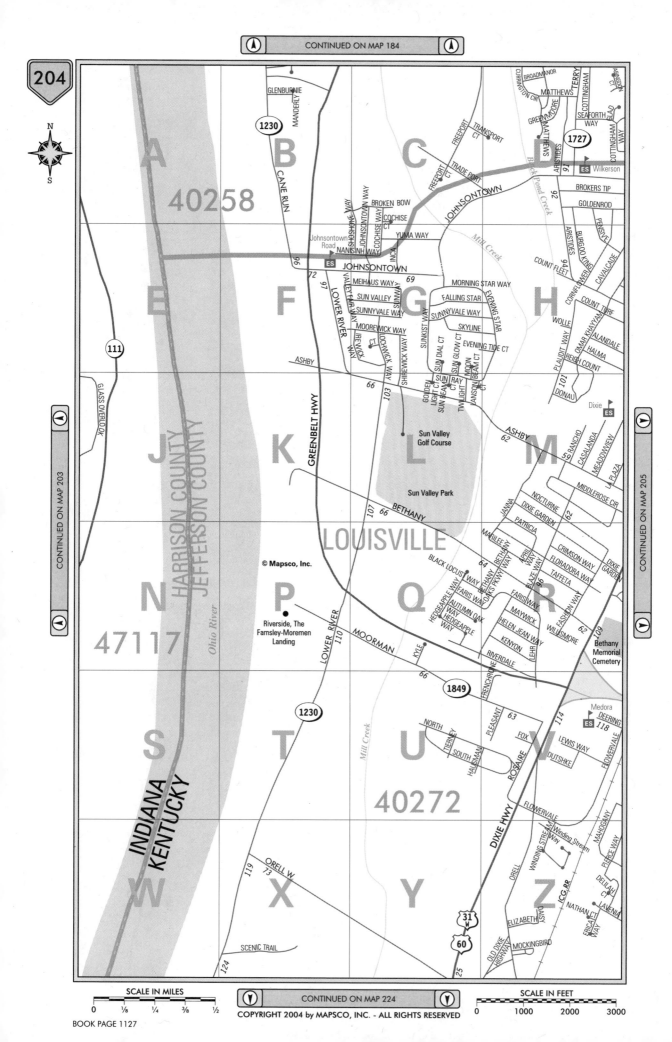

204

40258

40272

47117

LOUISVILLE

N

Ohio River

Mill Creek

Mill Creek

Buck Pond Creek

HARRISON COUNTY
JEFFERSON COUNTY

INDIANA
KENTUCKY

Sun Valley
Golf Course

Sun Valley Park

GLASS OVERLOOK

Riverside, The
Farmsley-Moremen
Landing

Bethany
Memorial
Cemetery

© Mapsco, Inc.

1230

1727

111

1230

1849

31

60

A B C
E F G H
J K L M
N P Q R
S T U V
W X Y Z

CONTINUED ON MAP 203
CONTINUED ON MAP 205

GLENBURNIE
MANDERLY
CANE RUN
JOHNSONTOWN WAY
JOHNSONTOWN Road
NANSINH WAY
BROKEN BOW
COCHISE
COCHISE CT
YUMA WAY
INCA
JOHNSONTOWN
MEIHAUS WAY
SUN VALLEY
SUNNYVALE WAY
MOOREWICK WAY
LOWER RIVER
VALLEY FAIR WAY
IREWICK WAY
LOCHWICK WAY
SHIREWICK WAY
SUNKIST WAY
ASHBY
GREENBELT HWY
FREEPORT CT
FREEPORT CT
TRANSPORT CT
TRADE PORT
JOHNSONTOWN
MORNING STAR WAY
FALLING STAR
EVENING STAR
SUNNYVALE WAY
SKYLINE
EVENING TIDE CT
SUN DIAL CT
SUN GLOW CT
SUN RAY CT
SUN BEAM CT
GOLDEN LIGHT CT
SUN BEAM
MOON
TWILIGHT
JANSON BEAM CT

BROADMANOR
CURRINGTON CIR
MATTHEWS
GRENNMOORE
MATTHEWS
TERRY
COTTINGHAM
SEAFORTH WAY
ARISTIDES
WILKERSON
COTTINGHAM RD
WAY
ARLINGTON
BROKERS TIP
GOLDENROD
ARISTIDES
BURGOO KING
CAVALCADE
PENSIVE
COUNT FLEET
CORNFLOWER WAY
COUNT TURF
WOLLE
PLAUDIT WAY
OMAR KHAYYAM
ALANDALE
HALMA
REIGH COUNT
DONAU
Dixie ES

ASHBY
ASHBY
RANCHO
CASALANDA
MEADOWVIEW
LA PLAZA
MIDDLEROSE CIR
NOCTURNE
DIXIE GARDEN
PATRICIA
JANNA
MARILEE
BETHANY
APRIL
BLAZE WAY
CRIMSON WAY
FLORADORA WAY
TAFETA
DIXIE GARDEN
BLACK LOCUST WAY
FARIS WAY
BETHANY
OAKS PKWY WAY
FARIS WAY
MAYWICK
WILLISMORE
FASHION WAY
HEDGEAPPLE WAY
AUTUMN OAK WAY
HEDGEAPPLE WAY
HELEN JEAN WAY
KENYON
LEHR
RIVERDALE
BETHANY

BETHANY
MOORMAN
LOWER RIVER
KYLE
FRENCHRIDGE
MEDORA ES
DEERING
NORTH
TIERNEY
SOUTH
HALESMAN
PLEASANT
FOX
ROSAIRE
LEWIS WAY
DUTSHKE
FLOWERVALE
FLOWERVALE
WINDING STREAM Way
WINDING STREAM
MAHOGANY
PIERCE WAY
DELILAH CT
LAVENIA
ERICA WAY
NATHAN CT
DAISY
ORELL
DIXIE HWY
ICG RR
OLD DIXIE HIGHWAY
ELIZABETH
MOCKINGBIRD
ORELL W
SCENIC TRAIL

CONTINUED ON MAP 224

SCALE IN MILES
0   1/8   1/4   3/8   1/2

SCALE IN FEET
0   1000   2000   3000

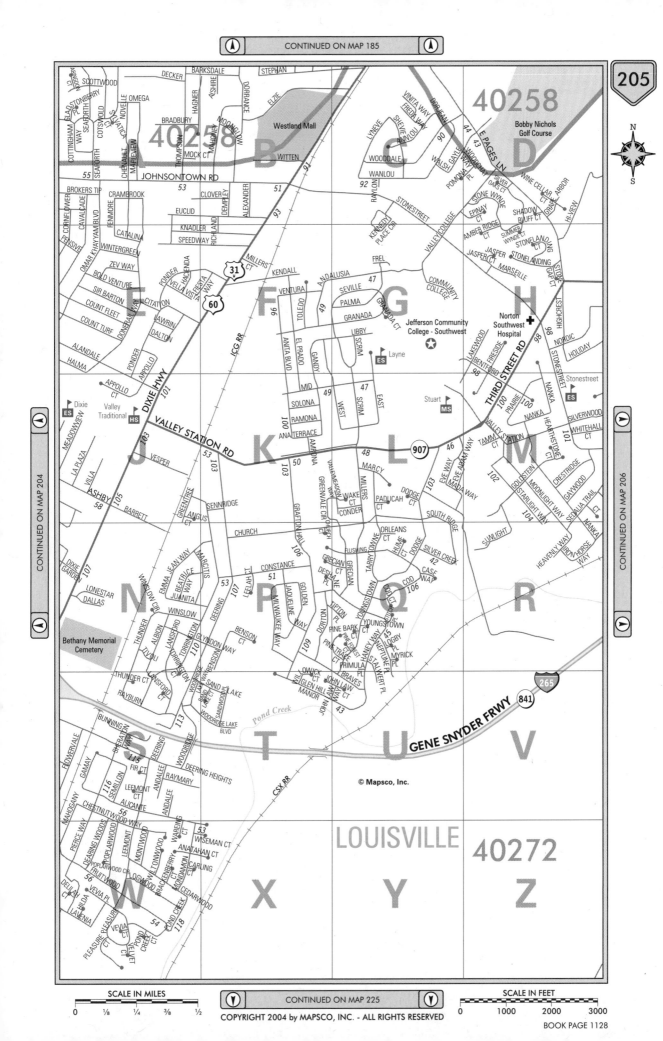

205

N
W S E
S

40258

40258

Bobby Nichols
Golf Course

Westland Mall

JOHNSONTOWN RD

Jefferson Community
College - Southwest

Norton
Southwest
Hospital

Community
College

DIXIE HWY

VALLEY STATION RD

THIRD STREET RD

Valley
Traditional

GENE SNYDER FRWY

265
841

Bethany Memorial
Cemetery

Pond Creek

LOUISVILLE

40272

© Mapsco, Inc.

CSX RR

CONTINUED ON MAP 204

CONTINUED ON MAP 206

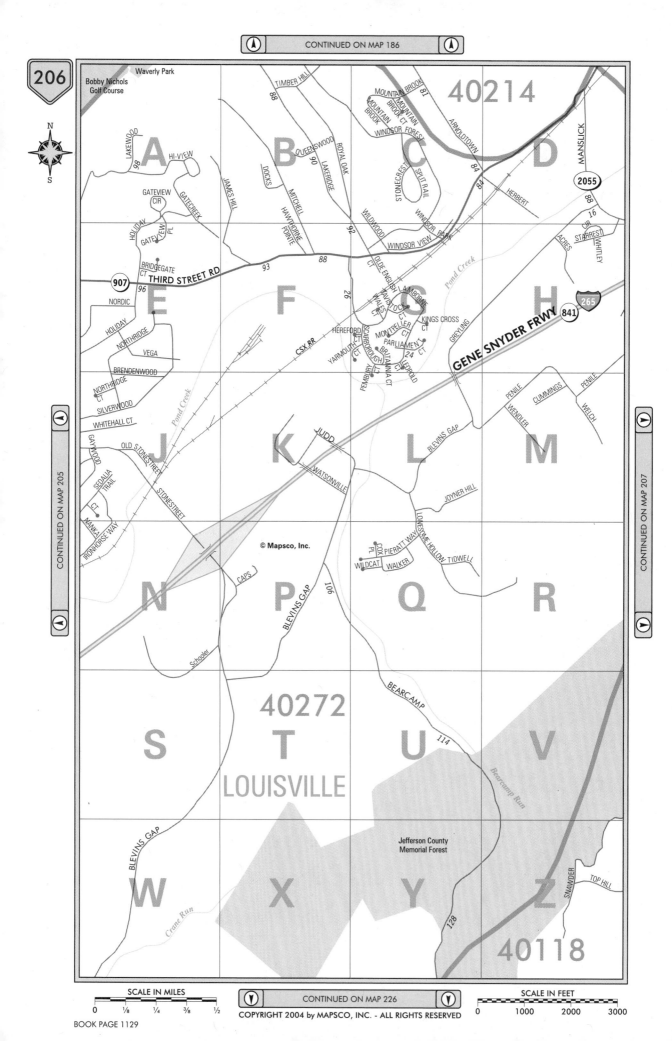

CONTINUED ON MAP 186

206

N
W E
S

Waverly Park
Bobby Nichols
Golf Course

40214

A

LAKEWOOD
HI-VIEW
GATEVIEW CIR
GATECREEK
HOLIDAY
GATEVIEW PL
98

JAMES HILL

B
TIMBER HILL
QUEENSWOOD
DOCKS
MITCHELL
HAWTHORNE POINTE
ROYAL OAK
LAKERIDGE
88
90

C
MOUNTAIN BROOK
MOUNTAIN BROOK CT
MOUNTAIN BROOK
WINDSOR FOREST
STONECREST
SPLIT RAIL
WILDWOOD
WINDSOR PARK
84
84
81
ARNOLDTOWN

D
MANSLICK
2055
HERBERT
88
16

BRIDGEGATE CT
907
96
THIRD STREET RD
93
92
88
WINDSOR VIEW

E
NORDIC
HOLIDAY
NORTHRIDGE
VEGA
BRENDENWOOD

F
26
CSX RR

G
OLDE ENGLISH
LAMBORNE
TAVISTOCK
WALES CT
HEREFORD
MONTPELIER
YARMOUTH CT
SCARBOROUGH CT
PEMBURY CT
BRITANNIA CT
PARLIAMENT
LEOPOLD
24
KINGS CROSS CT
GREYLING

H
GENE SNYDER FRWY
841
265

Pond Creek

ACRES
CIR
STARREST
WHITLEY

J
NORTHRIDGE CT
SILVERWOOD
WHITEHALL CT
GAYWOOD
OLD STONESTREET
SEDALIA TRAIL
NANKA CT
IRONHORSE WAY
STONESTREET

Pond Creek

K
JUDD
WATSONVILLE

L
BLEVINS GAP
JOYNER HILL
LONESOME HOLLOW

M
PENILE
WENDLER
CUMMINGS
PENILE
WELCH

© Mapsco, Inc.

N
CAPS
Schooler

P
BLEVINS GAP
106

Q
WILDCAT
COX PL
PIERATT WAY
WALKER
TIDWELL

R

BEARCAMP
114

S

T
40272

LOUISVILLE

U

Bearcamp Run

V

W
BLEVINS GAP
Crane Run

X

Y
Jefferson County
Memorial Forest
128

Z
SNAWDER
TOP HILL

40118

CONTINUED ON MAP 205
CONTINUED ON MAP 207

SCALE IN MILES
0   1/8   1/4   3/8   1/2

CONTINUED ON MAP 226

SCALE IN FEET
0   1000   2000   3000

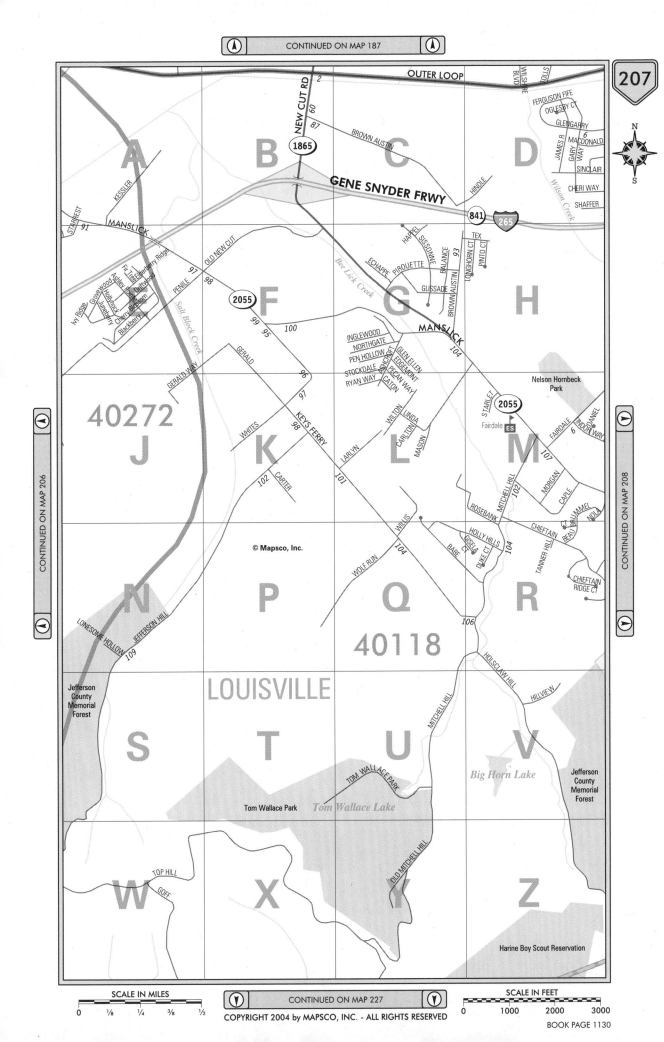

CONTINUED ON MAP 187

207

N
S

CONTINUED ON MAP 206

CONTINUED ON MAP 208

OUTER LOOP

NEW CUT RD

WILSHIRE BLVD

2

60

87

BROWN AUSTIN

A

B

C

D

FERGUSON FIFE
OGLESBY CT
GLENGARRY
JAMES R
MACDONALD
GARY WAY
SINCLAIR
CHERI WAY
SHAFFER
6

GENE SNYDER FRWY

1865

841 265

HINDLE

Wilson Creek

KESSLER

STARCREST

91

MANSLICK

HAPPEL
SISSONNE
ECHAPPE
PIROUETTE
BALANCE
BROWN AUSTIN
GLISSADE
LONGHORN CT
PINTO CT
TEX
93

Bee Lick Creek

Salt Block Creek

Ft. 116 Elderberry Ridge
Ashley Jone Driftwood
Grovewood Holmock
Ivy Ridge Junebarry
Cherry Blossom
Blackbarry

OLD NEW CUT
PENILE
97
98

2055

F

99
95
100

MANSLICK

104

G

H

INGLEWOOD
NORTHGATE
PEN HOLLOW
STOCKDALE
RYAN WAY
GLEN ELLEN
EDGEMONT
PECAN WAY
BISCHOFF
CATON

Nelson Hornbeck Park

40272

J

GERALD

GERALD WAY

96

97

WHITES

KEYS FERRY

98

K

WILTON
CARLTON
LARLYN
LINDA
MASON

L

STARLET

2055

Fairdale
ES

FAIRDALE
DANIEL
TINDOR WAY
6
107

M

102
CARTER

101

MITCHELL HILL
102
MORGAN
CARLE

ROSEBANK

WILLIS

WOLF RUN

104

HOLLY HILLS
GISELA CT
BABE
DUKE CT

CHIEFTAIN

BEAU BRUMMEL

NOLA

104

TANNER HILL

CHIEFTAIN RIDGE CT

N

LONESOME HOLLOW

JEFFERSON HILL

109

P

© Mapsco, Inc.

Q

40118

R

106

Jefferson County Memorial Forest

LOUISVILLE

S

T

HOLSCLAW HILL

HILLVIEW

MITCHELL HILL

U

Big Horn Lake

V

Jefferson County Memorial Forest

TOP HILL
GOFF

W

X

TOM WALLACE PARK

Tom Wallace Park   Tom Wallace Lake

OLD MITCHELL HILL

Y

Z

Harine Boy Scout Reservation

CONTINUED ON MAP 227

SCALE IN MILES
0   1/8   1/4   3/8   1/2

SCALE IN FEET
0   1000   2000   3000

BOOK PAGE 1130

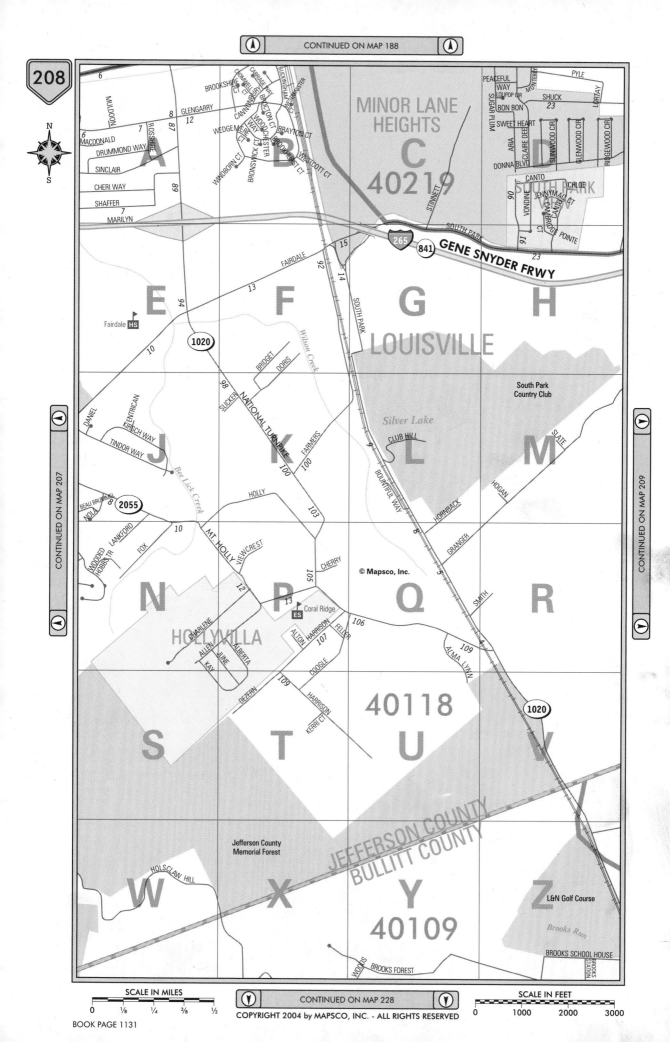

CONTINUED ON MAP 188

208

N
W E
S

6

MULDOON

MACDONALD 6   7
ROSSHIRE

DRUMMOND WAY   87
SINCLAIR   8   12
GLENGARRY

CHERI WAY   89

SHAFFER   7

MARILYN

A   B

BROOKSHIRE
CROMWELL CT
CABBAGE WAY
BROCTON CT
CANNONBURY
BUCKINGHAM SQ
BANNISTER

WEDGEMERE CT
WOODCHESTER
JACKMAN WAY   13
BRAYTON CT
PRESCOTT CT

WINDBORN CT
BRONSMAN
BROOKHURST CT

MINOR LANE
HEIGHTS

C
40219

STINNETT

PEACEFUL
WAY   PYLE
LOLIPOP CIR
MONTEREY
SUGAR PLUM
BON BON   SHUCK   23
SWEET HEART

ARIA
CLAIRE DEER   SUNWOOD CIR
GLENWOOD CIR
RIDGEWOOD CIR
DONNA BLVD   90   D

CANTO
CHLOE
JENNYMAC CT   SOUTH PARK
VONDINE   VIEW
CAMBRIDGE
CANTO
POINTE
91   CT   23

265   SOUTH PARK
841   GENE SNYDER FRWY

15

FAIRDALE   92   14
13

E   SOUTH PARK   G   LOUISVILLE   H
F

Fairdale HS

1020   10   94

BRIDGET   DORIS
Wilson Creek

South Park   South Park
Country Club

98
SLICKER   NATIONAL TURNPIKE

Silver Lake

CLUB HILL
SLATE

DANIEL
KENTRICAN   FARMERS
KIRSCH WAY   100   9   HORNBACK   HOGAN   M
TINDOR WAY   J   100   L
Bee Lick Creek

K   BOUNTIFUL WAY

BEAU BRUMMEL
NOLA   2055   8   HOLLY   103   GRANGER   8   R
WOODED   10   N   P   Q
LANKFORD   MT HOLLY   VIEWCREST   105   © Mapsco, Inc.   5
HOBBS TR   FOX   12   CHERRY   SMITH
13
Coral Ridge
ES   106   109
CHARLENE   HARRISON   ALMA LYNN
HOLLYVILLA   ALLEN   ALTON   FELLER   107
KAY   JUNE   ALBERTA   COOGLE   40118
DEZERN   109   U
S   HARRISON   T
KERRI CT

Jefferson County
Memorial Forest

JEFFERSON COUNTY
BULLITT COUNTY

1020

HOLSCLAW HILL   L&N Golf Course
W   X   Z

Brooks Run
Y
40109   BROOKS SCHOOL HOUSE

WOODS   BROOKS FOREST

CONTINUED ON MAP 207
CONTINUED ON MAP 209
CONTINUED ON MAP 228

SCALE IN MILES
0   1/8   1/4   3/8   1/2

SCALE IN FEET
0   1000   2000   3000

BOOK PAGE 1131

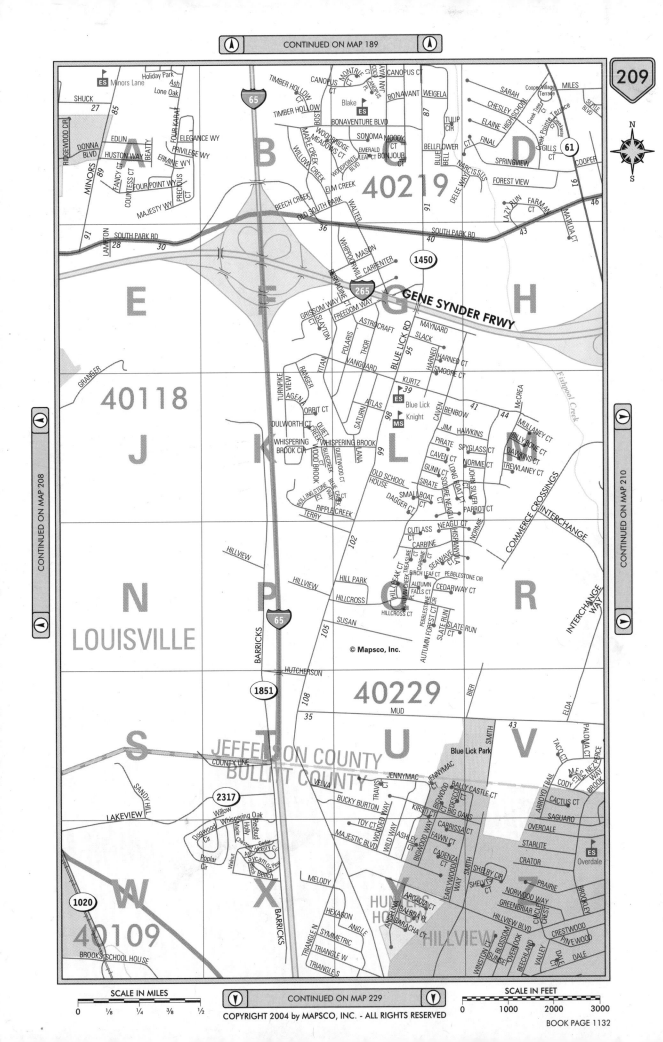

209

N
W E
S

CONTINUED ON MAP 208

CONTINUED ON MAP 210

40219

40118

LOUISVILLE

GENE SNYDER FRWY

40229

JEFFERSON COUNTY
BULLITT COUNTY

HILLVIEW

40109

© Mapsco, Inc.

SCALE IN MILES
0   1/8   1/4   3/8   1/2

SCALE IN FEET
0   1000   2000   3000

BOOK PAGE 1132

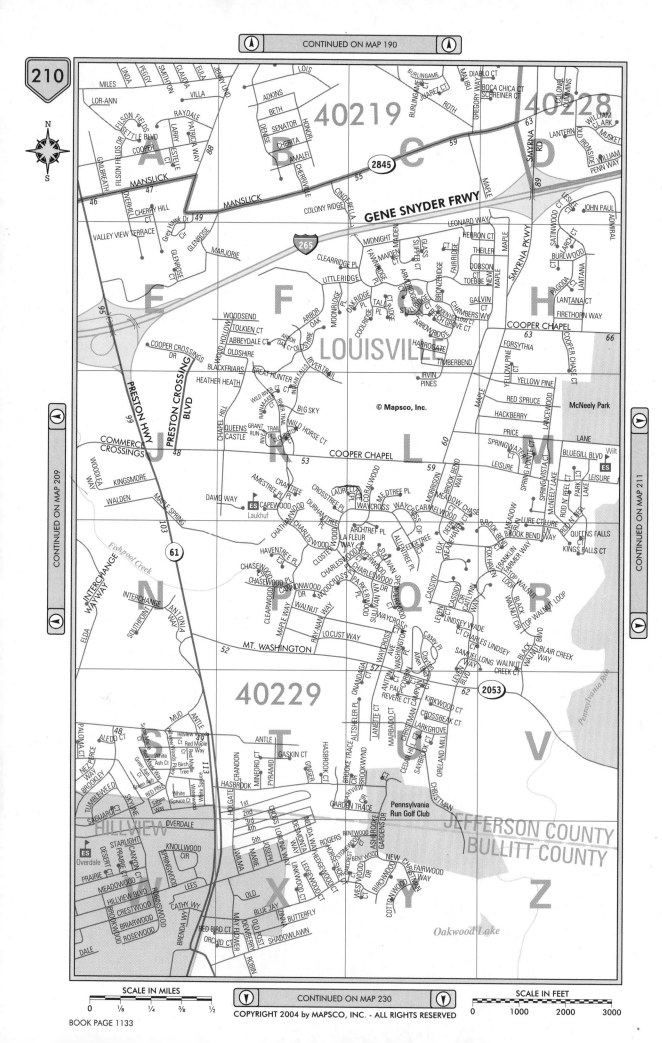

210

N
S

40219

40228

BURLINGAME
JUAREZ CT
MALIBU
DIABLO CT
BOCA CHICA CT
GREGORY WAY
SCHREINER CT
ROTH
COLONEL
CUMMINS

SMYRNA RD

WILLIAM CLARK
MUSKET
LANTERN
OLD IRONSIDE
WILLIAM PENN WAY

MILES
LINDA
PEGGY
SMITHTON
CLAUDIA
EULA
LOR-ANN
FILSON FIELDS
ELSETTLE BLVD
LARRY
RAYDALE
PATRICIA WAY
ESTELLE
JENNY LIND
VILLA
LOIS
ADKINS
BETH
DENISE
SENATOR
CHERITA
HONOR
AMALFI
CHERRIVILLE
88

A
B
C
D

GALBREATH
FILSON FIELDS
OVERHILL
COOPER
CHERRY HILL CT
MANSLICK
47
46
Grey Hawk Dr
Cir
49
CINDERELLA
COLONY RIDGE
55
2845
59
63
89
SMYRNA PKWY

GENE SNYDER FRWY

VALLEY VIEW TERRACE
GLENBOSE
GLENROSE CT
MARJORIE
265
CLEARRIDGE PL
LITTLERIDGE
MOONRIDGE
MIDNIGHT
FANNINRIDGE
MAIDEN
SLIPPER CT
SLV PL
ARNOLDRIDGE
CHAMBERS WY
STILLRIDGE
TALORIDGE
ARROWRIDGE
BRONZERIDGE
BEECH GROVE CT
HIDDENHOLLOW CT
GALVIN CT
LEONARD WAY
HERRON CT
THEILER
FAIRRIDGE CT
DOBSON CT
TOEBBE CT
NEW
MAPLE
MAPLE
SATINWOOD CT
LARCH CT
BURLWOOD
PAGODA
LANTANA
LANTANA CT
FIRETHORN WAY
LESLIE
JOHN PAUL
ADMIRAL

E
F
G
H

WOODSEND
TOLKIEN CT
ABBEYDALE CT
OLDSHIRE
BLACKFRIARS
HEATHER HEATH
ARBOR OAK
ARBOR OAK CT
OLDSHIRE
WOOD HOLLOW
OAK RIDGE PL
COOLRIDGE PL
HARROGATE
TIMBERBEND
COOPER CHAPEL
63
66
FORSYTHIA
YELLOW PINE
YELLOW PINE
RED SPRUCE
LANCEWOOD
HACKBERRY
McNeely Park

LOUISVILLE

RIVER TRAIL
GREAT HUNTER
INDIAN FALLS CT
WILD RIVER CT
RIVER TRAIL
BIG SKY
WILD HORSE CT
CLOVERTON
IRVIN PINES
© Mapsco, Inc.
MAPLE
PRICE
LANE
Wilt

PRESTON CROSSING BLVD
PRESTON HWY
COOPER CROSSINGS DR
CHAPEL HILL
QUEENS CASTLE
GRANT RUN
RAINMAKER CT
GRANT RUN CT
COOPER CHAPEL
53
60
SPRINGWATER CT
SPRING POINTE CT
LEISURE
SPRING VISTA CT
McNEELY LAKE
ROD N' REEL CT
PARK CT
ROD N' REEL
LAKE
BLUEGILL BLVD
LEISURE
ES

E
F
G
H
J
K
L
M

COMMERCE CROSSINGS
99
48
59
MORRISON
BROOK BEND
MEADOW CHASE
CARMELWOOD
BROOK BEND
MEADOW
ROBIN
LURE CT
LURE LN WAY
QUEENS FALLS CT
KINGS FALLS CT

WOODLEA WAY
KINGSMORE
WALDEN
MARBLE SPRING
103
DAVID WAY
AMESTREE PL
CRANTREE
CROSSTREE PL
CAPEWOOD
Laukhuf
ES
CHATHAMWOOD
DURHAMTREE
CHARLESWOOD
LAURELIA
WAYCROSS
WAYCROSS CIR
CORALWOOD
MEADTREE PL
ARCHTREE PL
LA FLEUR WAY
SHOPPERWOOD
ALLENTREE PL
SULLIVAN
SPENCERWOOD
EDGETREE
FOX
DEER HAVEN
MEADEHATCH CT
FRANKLIN
TEATOP WALNUT LOOP
BLACK WALNUT CIR

N
P
Q
R

61
Fishpool Creek
INTERCHANGE WAYWAY
INTERCHANGE WAY
ANTONIA WAY
SOUTHPOINT
HAVENTREE PL
CHASEWOOD
CHASEWOOD
CLEARWOOD CT
MAPLE WAY
CANNONWOOD DR
RAY-NAN WAY
CLOSTER PL
CHARLESWOOD
WOODCROSS PL
CHARLESWOOD PL
PARKEN
WOODCROSS
WALNUT WAY
LOCUST WAY
WAYCROSS
SUNDERWOOD
CASSIDY
LEVEN
LINDSEY WADE CT
CASSIDY
CAITLYNN
FOX HAVEN
CATLYNN
LINDSEY WADE
CHARLES LINDSEY
SAMUEL LONG WALNUT WAY
LEVEN BLVD
BLACK WALNUT BLVD
BLAIR CREEK WAY
CREEK CT

MT. WASHINGTON
52
ELDA
WAYCROSS AVE
WASHINGTON
ONANDAGA
57
Cassey Pl
CLAY PL
PAUL
ANTON
REVERE WAY
CAMPGRND
CHRISTMAN CAMPGRND
CORBIN
LEVEN
2053

40229

MUD
ANTLE
Hillview Woods Ct
Red Maple Way
ANTLE
GASKIN CT
GINGER
PALOMA CT
ALEDO CT
48
Green Ash Ct
White Ash Ct
49
Birch Tree
113
MINFORD CT
PYRAMID
HASBROOK CT
BROOKE TRACE
ALTSHELER PL
LANETTE CT
MARBADO CT
CHRISTMAN
KIRKWOOD CT
LARKGROVE
CROSSBEAK CT
ORELAND MILL
CHRISTMAN
CEDAR

S
T
U
V

NEZ PERCE WAY
BROKLEY
TUMBLEWEED
SAGUARO CT
SKYLINE
Red Pine Ct
Spruce Way
Green Ash Ct
White Spruce Ct
Sabine Way
HASBROOK
HOLGATE
CRANDON
1st
2nd
3rd
4th
5th
GARDEN TRACE
BROOKE TRACE CIR
BROOKWYND
Pennsylvania Run Golf Club
SAYBROOK CT
PARKVIEW CIR

HILLVIEW
Overdale
ES
OVERDALE
STARLIGHT
CANYON CT
KNOLLWOOD CIR
SPRINGWOOD
CROSS
DESMONTA WAY
RIDA WAY
LORONA WAY
ROGERS
BENTWOOD
DESMONTA
ASHBROOKE
GARDENS DR
CHRISTMAN
JEFFERSON COUNTY
BULLITT COUNTY
Pennsylvania Run

DESERT
PRAIRIE
MEADOWOOD
HILLVIEW BLVD
CRESTWOOD
BROOKWOOD
BRIARWOOD
ROSEWOOD
DALE
ROBINSWOOD
LEES
CATHY WY
BRENDA WY
OLD
RED BIRD CT
ORCHID CT
BLUE JAY
MAY FLOWERY
OLD POST
SHADOWLAWN
ROBIN
WILMA
MARIE
JOSEPH
LINKWOOD
LEDGEWOOD CT
LINKWOOD CT
ZINN
BUTTERFLY
DEWBERRY
PORSSTONE WAY
WESTWOOD CT
BENTWOOD
BIRCHWOOD
COTTONWOOD CT
FAIRWOOD DR
NEW CHRISTMAN
FAIRWOOD WAY
CREST WAY

W
X
Y
Z

Oakwood Lake

SCALE IN MILES
0   1/8   1/4   3/8   1/2
CONTINUED ON MAP 230
SCALE IN FEET
0   1000   2000   3000
BOOK PAGE 1133

CONTINUED ON MAP 209
CONTINUED ON MAP 211

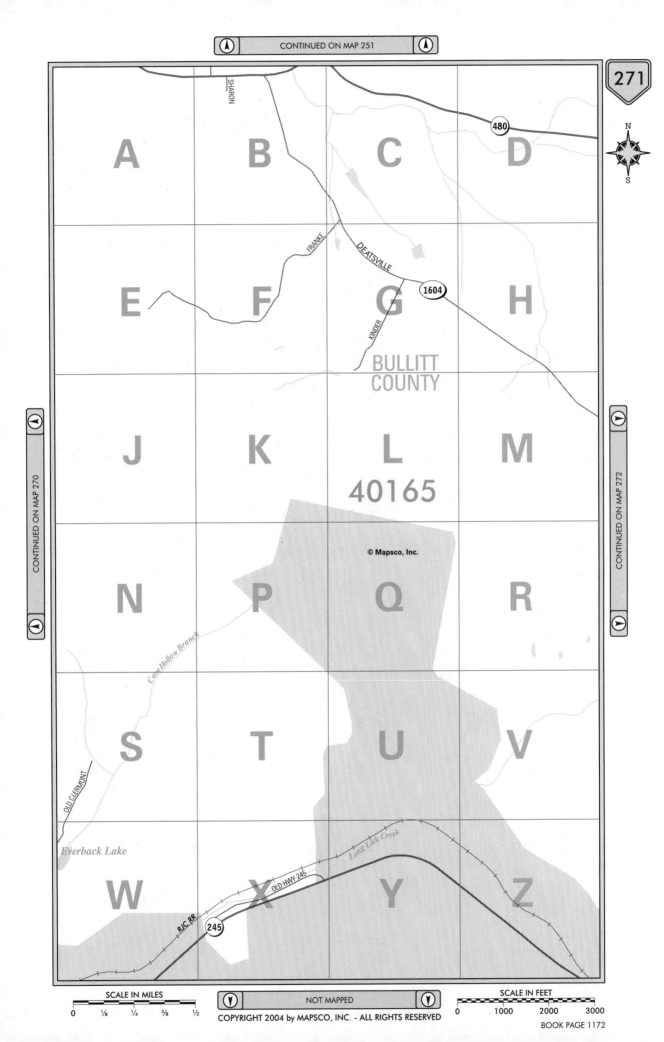

271

N
S

CONTINUED ON MAP 270

CONTINUED ON MAP 272

SHARON

480

FRANKE

DEATSVILLE

1604

KINDER

BULLITT
COUNTY

A B C D

E F G H

J K L M

40165

© Mapsco, Inc.

N P Q R

Cave Hollow Branch

S T U V

OLD CLERMONT

Everback Lake

Long Lick Creek

OLD HWY 245

W X Y Z

RJC RR

245

SCALE IN MILES
0   1/8   1/4   3/8   1/2

NOT MAPPED

SCALE IN FEET
0   1000   2000   3000

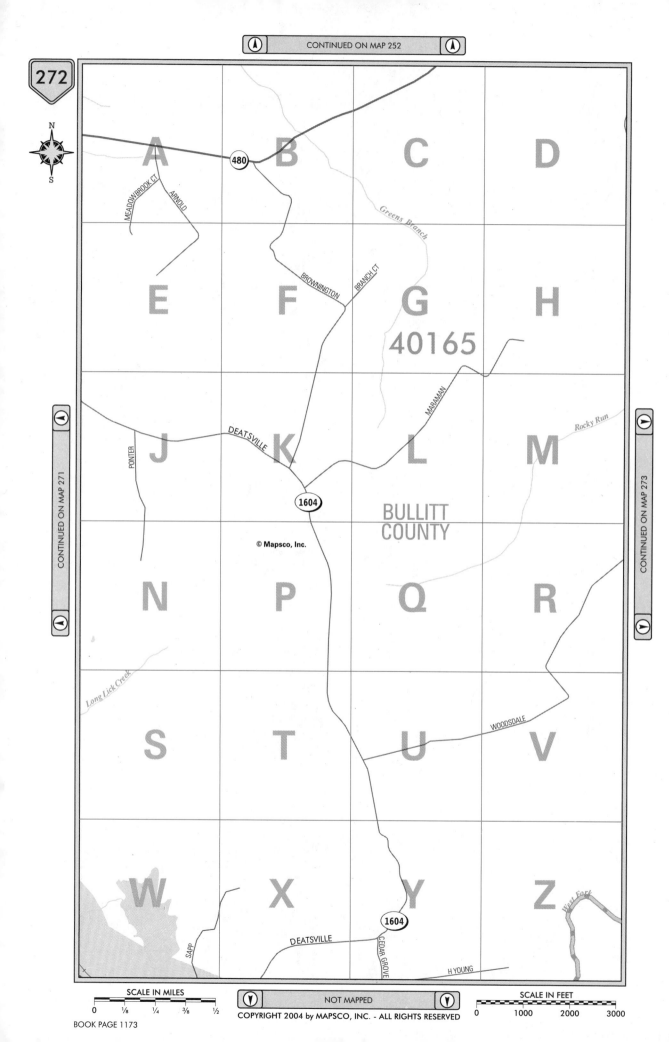

CONTINUED ON MAP 252

272

N
S

CONTINUED ON MAP 271

CONTINUED ON MAP 273

A

MEADOWBROOK CT

ARNOLD

480

B

C

D

Greens Branch

E

F

BROWNINGTON

BRANCH CT

G

40165

H

MARAMAN

Rocky Run

J

PONTER

DEATSVILLE

K

1604

© Mapsco, Inc.

L

M

BULLITT
COUNTY

N

P

Q

R

Long Lick Creek

S

T

U

WOODSDALE

V

W

X

Y

1604

DEATSVILLE

CEDAR GROVE

H YOUNG

Z

West Fork

SAPP

SCALE IN MILES

0   ⅛   ¼   ⅜   ½

NOT MAPPED

SCALE IN FEET

0   1000   2000   3000

BOOK PAGE 1173

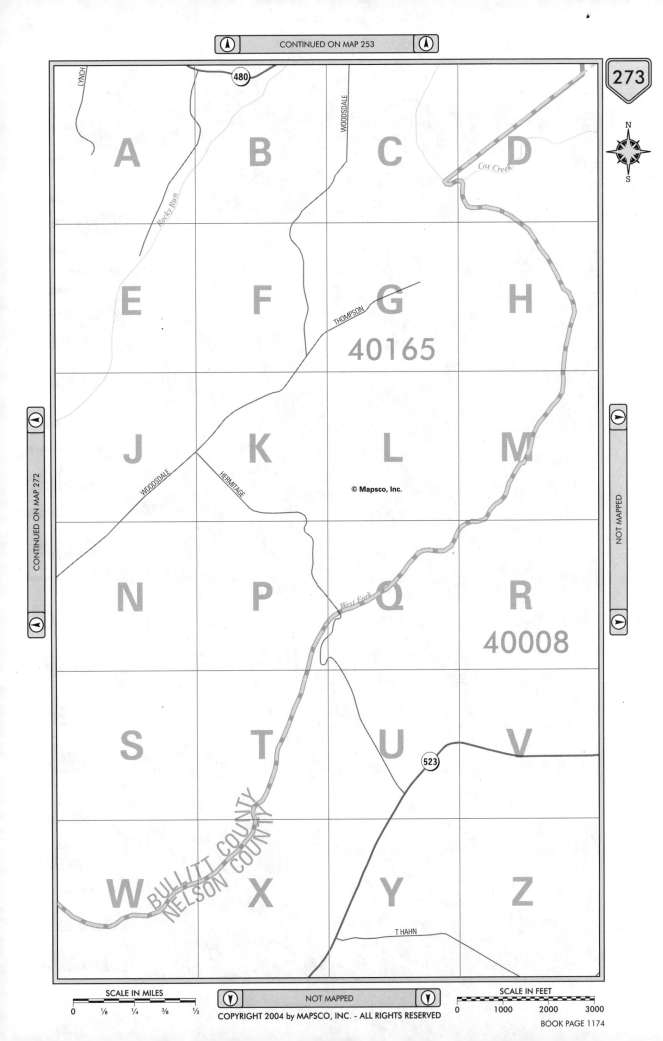

CONTINUED ON MAP 253

273

N
S

480

LYNCH

WOODSDALE

A

B

C

D

Cox Creek

E

F

THOMPSON

G

40165

H

CONTINUED ON MAP 272

J

WOODSDALE

K

HERMITAGE

L

© Mapsco, Inc.

M

NOT MAPPED

Rocky Run

N

P

West Fork

Q

R

40008

S

T

U

523

V

BULLITT COUNTY

NELSON COUNTY

W

X

Y

T HAHN

Z

NOT MAPPED

SCALE IN MILES

0   1/8   1/4   3/8   1/2

SCALE IN FEET

0   1000   2000   3000

COPYRIGHT 2004 by MAPSCO, INC. - ALL RIGHTS RESERVED

BOOK PAGE 1174